THE MIDDLE EAST
COMMANDOS

Charles Messenger
Colonel George Young DSO and
Lt-Colonel Stephen Rose OBE

Foreword by
General Sir John Hackett
GCB CBE DSO MC DL BLitt MA FRSL

WILLIAM KIMBER

© Charles Messenger, George Young, Stephen Rose 1988

All rights reserved. No part of this publication may be
reproduced, stored in a retrieval system or transmit-
ted, in any form or by any means, electronic,
mechanical, photocopying, recording or otherwise,
without prior permission in writing from William
Kimber & Co Limited.

First published in 1988

British Library Cataloguing in Publication Data

Messenger, Charles, *1941 –*
The Middle East commandos.
1. World War   2. Middle Eastern campaigns.
Army operations by Great Britain. Army.
Middle East Commandos
I. Title   II. Young, George   III. Rose, Stephen
940.54′23

ISBN 0-7183-0645-7

William Kimber & Co Limited is part of the
Thorsons Publishing Group, Wellingborough,
Northamptonshire, NN8 2RQ, England.

Printed in Great Britain by Redwood Burn Limited,
Trowbridge, Wiltshire.

1 3 5 7 9 10 8 6 4 2

Contents

FOREWORD
by
General Sir John Hackett GCB CBE DSO MC DL BLitt MA FRSL

It is probably in large part due to the offshore location of these islands, looking out on a great ocean inviting ship passage to the very end of the earth, that the history of their inhabitants over the centuries has been so closely linked to the sea. The restless urge of islanders the world over to move beyond their islands has rarely been more marked than in the group lying off the north-west coast of Europe, no part of which lies at the furthest more than a few score miles from the sea. These people had had no common land frontier with a continental neighbour since the loss of the last French possessions of the English crown in the sixteenth century, and by the mid-twentieth had not experienced effective invasion for close on a thousand years. The mixed racial origins of the islanders, secure behind their sea barrier, contributed to a highly detached and independent outlook, while their close associations with the sea led them naturally to maritime adventure and, in war, to the exploitation of the indirect approach. Where there was blue water there was an open flank and the habit of seeking and using it would find application where there were other natural barriers too, such as deserts.

Inevitably, with Britain thrust out of an axis-dominated Europe in 1940 but determined, under stout hearted leadership, to fight on if necessary alone, thoughts turned at once to the possibility of taking the war to the enemy in seaborne raids. Thus was born the Commando concept, out of which grew the high and complex variety of raiding operations in which Britain made such a characteristic and notable contribution to the waging of the Second World War.

It was the urgent need to foster an offensive outlook which chiefly weighed with Churchill in ordering, in June 1940, the raising of special raiding forces on a considerable scale, making use of experience already gained in the gallant but ill-fated campaign in Norway. Quite apart from the need to project offensive operations from Britain, however, there was also the vulnerability of the British position in the Mediterranean and the Middle East to be considered, and it was in fact to be in this area that the raiding operations of our special forces, in so many different modes, would be most effective.

Much has been written since the war ended about the operations of Commandos and other special forces. Such spectacularly different but, each in its own way, highly successful units as the LRDG and Stirling's SAS, and George Jellicoe's Special Boat Squadron, have received well deserved attention. So has the unit I myself, as GSO1 Raiding Forces in HQ MEF in late 1942, raised under the official name of No 1 Long Range Demolition Squadron, with the pet name I invented for it of 'Popski's Private Army', which stuck. Popski claimed in Vienna after the war that I had invented him too but that would be going too far.

There were other less well publicised groups, like the Greek Sacred Squadron, the Greek Spongefishers who knew the inner Sirte so well, the Kalpacks – Turkish speaking assassins under a Greek epigraphist from Edinburgh University kept on ice to do away with German generals if they ever came down through the Caucasus – and so on. The circus handed to me in the newly created G OPS Branch called 'Raiding Forces', when I was brought in unwillingly from the Desert to pick up the pieces after the disastrous Tobruk raid in September 1942, was a fascinating one, if a trifle odd.

The extraordinary thing about Commandos in the Middle East, however, is that in the whole time, nearly half a century, since the end of the war, the Commando units actually raised and used in that theatre have never until now been the subject of a book written specifically about them. This has now at least been put right and the result of much painstaking work done for the Middle East Commandos Historical Research Group, by Colonel G.A.D. Young DSO and Lieutenant-Colonel S.M. Rose OBE, is now, with the notable assistance of Charles Messenger, put before the public in this book.

Under orders from the War Office three Commandos were raised by GHQ Middle East in the last half of 1940. Two, Nos. 50 and 52, were made up of volunteers from British Regular and Yeomanry regiments already in the theatre, with a sprinkling of South African and Rhodesians and an unusual component in some 70 Spaniards who had fought against Franco and had to leave Spain when he came to power. No. 51, raised in the British mandated territory of Palestine, had the unique distinction of embodying both Jews, to about 60 per cent, and Arabs, in a unit whose distinguished performance in Abyssinia, Eritrea and the Western Desert showed the harmony possible between Jew and Arab before Zionist excesses after the war destroyed any further chance of it for ever. This Commando was more actively employed and longer lived than either of the other two. These were, after many vicissitudes, put together to form D Battalion of Layforce in Crete and fought a most gallant rearguard action covering the evacuation of the island. This was to leave almost all their own number behind on Crete as prisoners of war.

The almost complete loss of two out of three ME Commandos in that summer of 1941 was a prelude to a period of uncertainty and confusion over the structure, command and organisation of special forces, now seen to be of more and more importance in the theatre, from which Middle East Commandos would never, as fully fledged entities, again emerge. The disbandment of No. 51 after the fall of Gondar in November 1941 virtually brought their short life to an end, though officers and men drawn from them would play a considerable part in further raiding operations under other command. The climax of this period of confusion was to be the costly disaster of the Tobruk raid in September 1942, in which elements out of 51 Commando played a gallant part in what was for them a total tragedy. The Tobruk operation was too ambitious, too complex and mounted with appalling insecurity and, incredible as it sounds, no single commander. All it had in the way of command was an interservice committee. The need for a thorough reorganisation in the theatre was now clear. GHQ sought to meet it by setting up a new G OPS Section under a GSO1 who was to be an officer snatched, much against his will, out of an armoured regiment in the Desert, where he was very happy, to be given as his first task the picking up of the pieces after the Tobruk disaster. Thereafter he was to try to rationalise the kaleidoscope of special forces without diminishing the priceless individuality of the men in them. That officer was myself, quite soon to go on from this truly enchanting circus to raise a parachute brigade.

It was sadly then too late, however, to save the Commandos. The mould had been broken and could not now be refashioned. New patterns were emerging while shortage of manpower prevented any but the most sparing use of men, where only the best would do, extracted from regiments unwilling to lose them. The War Establishment agreed for Popski's unit, for example, five officers and only eighteen men, no more. I was to see a good deal of Harry Cator during this time of reorganisation but with the best will in the world could not wave a wand and recreate what had gone. The opportunity to recall an exciting world which passed into limbo nearly a half a century ago made me glad to accept the invitation to write this piece into a book which should have appeared long before now. It is at least a book which has been written while there are still those around who can enrich from personal experience the ample documentary evidence that is available.

This is an important and valuable book not as a triumphant chronicle of continuous and brilliant success but as something of greater value. It is a record of experience in a highly important area of warfare whose importance has not grown less, with lessons not to be disregarded. It is also a record of the actions in war of brave, determined, dedicated men whom no amount of frustration and discouragement could turn away from the exacting path they had chosen and who have hitherto received little of the recognition they so richly deserve. The telling of their story will now do something at least to put the record straight.

Introduction

Books about Special Forces in the Second World War, especially the Commandos, are legion and continue to be published. Few, however, have made any mention of the Middle East Commandos, and what scattered references there are have been largely inaccurate and for the most part disparaging. It was because of this that, under the inspiration of the late Arthur Noble, a few survivors of the Middle East Commandos got together in 1981 under the leadership of Colonel George Young and Lt-Colonel Stephen Rose to pool their memories, forty years after the disbandment of the original Middle East Commandos.

This was the Middle East Commando Historical Research Group (MECHRG), a list of whose members is given at Appendix VI. Their recollections, combined with research in the Public Record Office and elsewhere, resulted in the gathering of a wealth of material. This has now been organised as the MECHRG Papers, which are to be presented to the National Army Museum.

In the meantime, in 1984, while researching for his book *The Commandos 1940–1946*, Charles Messenger had been put in touch with the MECHRG by one of its members, William Seymour. He himself was also writing a book on Special Forces in the Second World War, in which the Middle East Commandos were finally to receive the acknowledgement due to them. Gradually, the idea evolved that the ME Commandos' history should be published in book form. Here, thanks to William Kimber & Co Ltd, is the result.

There are, however, a number of individuals, other than members of the MECHRG, to whom the authors wish to give thanks. Henry Brown MBE, Secretary to the Commando Association for many years, has been of much help in tracking down former ME Commandos. Useful advice was given by Dr Peter Thwaites of the Imperial War Museum and David Smurthwaite of the National Army Museum. We are most grateful to the late Major-General F.C.C. Graham CB DSO for allowing us to quote from his paper *Cretan Crazy Week*. The late and highly eminent naval historian Captain Stephen Roskill gave most helpful comment on the Castelorizzo operation. Likewise, Brigadier Michael Blackman OBE

MC gave useful information on the part played by the Sherwood Foresters in the same operation. Senor Daniel Arasa of Madrid threw light on the Spanish Troop of No. 50 ME Commando. Colonel Ken Wylie DSO MBE provided information on the part played by A Battalion Layforce during the Battle for Crete. We thank, too, John Cator very much for allowing us to use his father's diaries. Finally, we deeply appreciate the kindness of General Sir John Hackett GCB CBE DSO MC DL BLitt MA FRSL in writing the foreword.

George Young
Stephen Rose
Charles Messenger

CHAPTER ONE

Formation

On 10 June 1940, Mussolini announced that Italy would consider herself at war with Britain and France from the following day. For the French, with the northern half of their country already totally overrun by the Germans, this made little difference, apart from the fact that the Italians shortly afterwards launched an invasion of the French Riviera. It also posed no additional threat to Britain herself, but to her sphere of influence in the Middle East it most certainly did. Large Italian forces in Libya, Abyssinia and Eritrea threatened the British possessions in East Africa, as well as Egypt and, most important of all, the Suez Canal. There was also the shadow of the Italian fleet lying over Britain's freedom of maritime manoeuvre in the Mediterranean. To face this there was the Mediterranean Fleet and little more than 30,000 troops and not too many aircraft, almost all of which were obsolescent types.

Britain herself now faced the prospect of a German cross-Channel invasion, but as early as 3 June 1940, conscious of the need to foster an offensive spirit, Churchill had given orders to the Chiefs of Staff to pay urgent attention to the setting up of raiding forces to carry out operations on the coasts of Occupied Europe. By the end of that month the Commando concept had come into being, but it was to apply not only to the forces now defending Britain, but also to those in the Middle East.

As irregular operations were the responsibility of the Military Intelligence (Research) (MI(R)) branch of the War Office, so GHQ Middle East Forces (MEF) also had an MI(R) branch run by Colonel Adrian Simpson. He was responsible for the organisation of native irregulars for operations in enemy-held territory and, towards the end of June 1940, the Long Range Desert Group, which was then in the process of being formed, came under his wing. He was now tasked with raising a Middle East Commando. His proposals for this were approved on 29 June and the next few weeks were spent in bringing these proposals to fruition.

The actual task of forming the Middle East Commando fell on two officers. The first of these was Major George Young, a Sapper officer, who was second-in-command of MI(R) Branch GHQ MELF. He had been one of the founder members of MI(R) in the War Office, when it had been set up, originally as General Staff (Research) Branch under Lt-Colonels Joe Holland and Colin Gubbins (later to head the Special Operations Executive), in spring 1939.

Just before the outbreak of war, George Young had been sent to the Middle East, together with some half dozen temporary commissioned officers to begin initiating and training for various projects. The most notable of these was a plan to destroy the Rumanian oilfields, which had originally been drawn up in July 1939. A field company Royal Engineers, then stationed in Egypt, was selected to carry out the task, and George Young himself paid a clandestine visit to Rumania in December 1939 and established contact with British engineers working there. In May 1940 permission was obtained from the Turkish Government to move the field company to Chanak, which had been selected as the jump-off point, and the sappers were sent there in civilian clothes, ostensibly to assist the Turks in improving the roads and harbour installations in the area. The fall of France, however, completely altered the situation, with Rumania now showing increasing sympathy for the Axis and Turkey becoming more sensitive over her neutrality. The plan therefore had to be abandoned and the company returned to Egypt. George Young was still under attachment from the War Office when he was called upon to raise the first Middle East Commando.

To assist him, he was joined in MI(R) on 6 July by Captain Harry Fox-Davies of the Durham Light Infantry. Fox-Davies had been interested in irregular operations for some years. As a very young subaltern, in 1935, he had had the temerity to address a letter to his then divisional commander, using the good offices of his ADC, Bernard Fergusson, later of Chindit fame and Governor-General of New Zealand. The formation was 2nd Infantry Division, and its commander was none other than Major-General A.P. Wavell, now Commander-in-Chief MELF.

Fox-Davies queried the concept that the enemy could only be defeated in 'formal battle' and argued that much more thought should be given to 'destroying the "brains", that is the commanders and headquarters, from within', as well as his supplies and means of communication. This could be done by using 'well trained guerilla troops'.[1] Wavell had sympathy with these ideas and, indeed, allowed Fox-Davies to try them out during the Army manoeuvres of 1936. They were so successful that, to the annoyance of the directing staff, but delight of the troops taking part, the exercise was brought to a premature end. Fox-Davies, who must be regarded as one of the pioneers of the Commando concept, now had the opportunity to see his ideas put into action against a real enemy, or so he hoped.

By mid-July 1940 a provisional establishment for what was to become No. 50 Middle East Commando had been approved. In essence, it was to be made up of a headquarters and three troops, each of four sections. A section would consist of one officer and 25 NCOs and men, and the total strength of the Commando was 371 all ranks, with an RAMC doctor and three orderlies, RAOC armourer sergeant and two interpreters attached. Apart from the attached personnel, all ranks were to be volunteers, but no one was allowed to be recruited from engineer or armoured units, or, for that matter, from any of the technical corps. Furthermore, although no commanding officer could stop a man from volunteering, each battalion or regiment was restricted from providing more than two officers and eight men.

The consequence of all this was that volunteers came principally from the infantry battalions stationed in the Middle East and from the still horsed 1st Cavalry Division in Palestine. Nevertheless, there were still too many volunteers for the numbers required. This was understandable, given that many units had been in the Middle East for some months on a war footing, but had as yet seen no action and even now the Italians in Libya seemed remarkably hesitant about launching their expected invasion of Egypt. A further problem was that there was at the time a severe shortage of equipment in the theatre, which meant that a brake had to be placed on recruitment, since there was initially only sufficient to train one troop. It also quickly became clear that no allowance in the establishment had been made for the inevitable administrative duties, and this, especially the lack of a quartermaster, placed a severe burden in the early days on George Young and his adjutant.

At this stage (end of July 1940), another manpower factor, and unique at that, rose to the surface. There had recently arrived in Palestine a number of Spaniards, who had escaped across the border from French mandated Syria. Theirs was a singular story. They had originally fought on the Republican side in the Spanish Civil War of 1936–39 and when General Franco had finally achieved victory they had fled across the Pyrenees and into France. In September 1939 they had joined the French Army, determined to continue the fight against Fascism, and were originally to be sent to help the Poles, but the country had been overrun before they could go. Instead they were sent to Syria, the majority as members of the 11th Bataillon du Marche, but some to the French Foreign Legion.

On the fall of France and the establishment of the Vichy Government, to which the French authorities in Syria declared their loyalty, the Spaniards became fearful for their safety. They had made no secret of their left wing political sympathies and feared that the Germans might clandestinely take control of Syria, in which case their future would be bleak. Their French officers warned them of what might happen and so, taking their weapons and two 3-ton Cameon trucks, they managed to get across the border with Palestine. They told the British that they wanted to fight on, but only under British officers and as British soldiers.

This understandably created problems within GHQ MELF as to what to do with them, and it was that, given their previous experience of active service and obvious resilience, some at least could be enlisted into the Middle East Commandos. Consequently, on 31 July, George Young and Harry Fox-Davies went to Moascar, a garrison on the Suez Canal, and interviewed the Spaniards. In all, there were 63 of them, and the lot were accepted. They were told to elect four of their brethren to be section commanders and these were given the rank of probationary corporal. In order to legalise their position they were badged as members of The Queen's Royal Regiment (West Surrey).

The Middle East Commando itself began to form at Geneifa during the first week of August 1940. Among the early arrivals was Captain Stephen Rose, who would later become second-in-command of No. 50 ME Commando. His experience was typical of many of the volunteers. He had been serving abroad with his battalion for the past four years, first in India and now in Egypt, and was a 26-year-old company commander. He had become increasingly frustrated by the endless manoeuvres, which seemed to consist largely of digging practice weapon pits and then filling them in again. Furthermore, there appeared to be little scope for individual initiative, and the Middle East Commandos provided a heaven-sent opportunity for him and other more adventurous non-conformists to satisfy their desire for action.

As a matter of policy, the volunteers of each regiment were kept together in the same section. While this produced a 'clannish' character, which might have acted against the cohesion of the Commando as a whole, it did not. Because Commando operations were built round the small group, individual regimental esprit de corps acted for the best in that the sub-sections had close cohesion from the outset.

Since the Mediterranean provided the Italians in Libya with a long open left flank, the original primary role of the ME Commandos was seen as raiding operations against the enemy coastline, as it was for the UK-based Commandos. The possibility was also seen of infiltration through the front line in order to strike at supply dumps and airfields in the enemy's rear, a task which would later become the speciality of the Special Air Service (SAS) and, to a lesser extent, the LRDG. In order to prepare the Commandos for this much specialised training was required. There was, however, an urgent need to get the Commandos operational as soon as possible, and a six weeks' syllabus was evolved, an outline of which is given at Appendix I.

Physical fitness and endurance were obviously of vital importance, and a standard was laid down which had to be achieved by each man. This was to be able to cover 30 miles cross-country on foot in 24 hours for three successive days, with a fixed amount of food and water. Naturally, at first it was difficult to control the consumption of both and there was a desire to eat and drink all they had early on. As a result very rigorous discipline was enforced and it became an offence for any man to eat or drink without orders from the officer or NCO in charge of the party.

Much emphasis was placed on night work, and the overall policy on movement in extreme heat was to lie up by day and move and carry out operations at night, when it was cooler. Most endurance exercises were carried out following this pattern. Thus, a typical one carried out by No. 50 involved marching to Port Suez and there embarking in the ABV *Saggita*, which belonged to the manufacturer of Branston Pickles. After landing on the coast of the Red Sea, the Commando then marched back to Geneifa, carrying out schemes and practice demolitions on the way, the whole lasting for three days.

All sorts of experiments were carried out with rations. These were based on the assumption that each man might well be away from his base for up to four days and had to be able to carry food for this length of time on his person. Thus, where possible, concentrated foods were used, although efforts in introducing dried meat – South African *billtong* on which the Boer commandos of 40 years earlier had subsisted so successfully – were not a success. Ration beef, which had been kept in cold store for months, did not dry well and there was strong consumer resistance. Thus, this idea had to be abandoned. Eventually, a typical 24-hour ration was as follows:

1 full water bottle
2oz rice
4oz dates
2oz sugar
3/4oz tea
6oz bully beef
4oz biscuits
2pkts chewing gum
4 limes

In addition, vitamin tablets were included. As an experiment, which was also being carried out in Britain at this time, Benzedrine was also issued, especially for use by sentries when lying up after a long march. Each man also had a water purification kit, the assumption being that he would be able to replenish his water bottle from local sources.

Watermanship was also considered very important, both from the point of view of amphibious operations and also for crossing water obstacles. Unlike the UK-based Commandos, there were no specialised landing craft in the Middle East at this time and, indeed, few enough in Britain. The ME Commandos therefore had to make do with ships' whalers and, to cross obstacles, improvised rafts. Amphibious training took place on the Great Bitter Lakes and the ships' boats used were provided with wooden bungs and mallets in order to plug leaks caused by bullet holes. Training in demolitions was designed to enable all ranks to be able to prepare and fire simple explosive charges, using the standard issue blocks of gun cotton and safety fuses. In the event, there was not enough time to train everyone in this, although later on this was made good and eventually everyone could set charges in the dark and under water.

Many of the early volunteers were regular soldiers, some with years of service, and they were used to the parade ground discipline of the peacetime Army. Something more was needed, however, to make a man a good commando. Greater stress had to be placed on the individual. Thus, in order to encourage a greater degree of independence of thought and action, especially when faced with the unexpected, it was decided to dispense with drill parades and saluting within unit lines, although strict punctuality and high standards of individual personal behaviour were insisted on when off duty. In order to further encourage the Commando spirit private soldiers were given the rank of Raider. This 're-education' was not wholly successful, especially when it came to the formation of No. 52 ME Commando, as we shall see, and it took time for some men to adapt. The Spaniards, on the other hand, proved to be remarkably amenable to this form of discipline, and having their own NCOs contributed much towards this. There was, however, not the time to ensure that these NCOs would be really effective in action and for this reason they came to rely heavily on their British officers.

Another significant difference from their UK-based counterparts was that it was not possible to foster individual self-discipline and self-reliance by paying each man ration and lodging allowance and making him find his own accommodation. Suitable civilian billets simply did not exist in Egypt, and hence the ME Commandos were forced to live in a conventional camp.

Another aspect which needed much experimentation before the right answer was found was dress. The normal uniform of the MELF, shorts, hosetops and ammunition boots quickly proved itself to be totally impracticable when it came to stalking and operating over rough desert terrain. Eventually, loose-fitting khaki drill trousers, with webb anklets and boots resoled using condemned motor tyres, were adopted. These were worn with a bush jacket and the Australian slouch hat, although steel helmets were usually worn when in action.

Rather than the straightforward Commando knife, the Middle East Commandos adopted their own form of specialist weapon, a knife-cum-knuckleduster known affectionately as the 'Fanny'. This was modelled on a smaller but similar weapon found in the Cairo Police Museum and was tested using animal carcasses in the Royal Army Service Corps supply depot at Abbassia. The Fanny also made up the distinctive cap badge of the Middle East Commandos, although purposely made very small so as not to be too distinctive. As for more conventional weapons, officers were armed with pistols, as were warrant officers and sergeants, who also had Tommy guns when these were available. The junior ranks had the standard service rifle of the time, the Short Magazine Lee Enfield (SMLE) with long bayonet, apart from Bren gun teams who also had pistols. Mechanical transport was virtually non-existent and this, together with the lack of administrative staff, meant that the ME Commandos were totally reliant on other units for resupply and transport when in action, which did have its disadvantages.

Likewise, operational difficulties were compounded by an almost complete absence of wireless sets.

The first part of No. 50 ME Commando, one troop and the Spaniards, completed their training on 5 October. By now George Young had been promoted to lieutenant-colonel and Harry Fox-Davies major and second-in-command. In the meantime, the war in the Middle East had become more active. On 4 August, Italian troops had invaded British Somaliland and quickly overrun the small British garrison there, as well as making small encroachments into Sudan. Then, on 13 September 1940, the Tenth Italian Army began its long awaited invasion of Egypt from Libya. Wavell, instead of trying to resist the Italians on the frontier, preferred to husband his greatly inferior strength and withdrew in the face of the Italian advance. As it happened, this came to a halt after three days, some 60 miles from the frontier, and the Italians set about building a series of fortified camps.

Wavell now enacted a policy of harassment while he awaited the arrival of reinforcements from Britain. It was natural that, in order to help carry this out, eyes should turn towards the Middle East Commandos. While as early as 12 September, the day before the Italians crossed into Egypt, a meeting at GHQ MELF had agreed that the Commandos in Egypt should be expanded to four British and three Indian, there was only part of No. 50 ME Commando actually immediately available for operations by early October. Nevertheless, in the middle of this month George Young was given a warning order for an operation.

The Gulf of Bomba lies between Tobruk and Derna on the Libyan coast. Here the Italians had established a seaplane base and, although it had been successfully attacked by the Fleet Air Arm in August, it was decided to use No. 50 to carry out another raid on it with the object of inflicting maximum damage. Planning for this was carried out by George Young, Harry Fox-Davies and the captains of the destroyers HMS *Decoy* and *Hereward*, which were to transport the commandos to their objective, under the overall direction of the Flag Officer Submarines.

Good maps and air photographs were available and a specially secure briefing tent was set aside at Geneifa. With the information available, it was possible to build a replica of Bomba on the shores of the Great Bitter Lakes, using tapes and latrine screens. The plan which evolved was for the commandos to land at about midnight and head for the huts and tents which contained the Italian garrison. These were to be destroyed with incendiary grenades, while the garrison itself was to be subjected to automatic fire and grenades. In the meantime, Royal Navy motor boats would go up and down the lines of moored seaplanes, using incendiary rockets to destroy them. Once maximum damage had been inflicted to these and the shore installations, the commandos would be withdrawn and re-embarked. Numerous rehearsals were carried out on the replica and by the end every man was thoroughly familiar with the lay-out in darkness and knew exactly what he had to do.

On the night of 27/28 October, *Decoy* and *Hereward* moored in the Great Bitter Lakes and embarked the Commando. The ships then set sail for Port Said. Once dawn arrived, all commandos were ordered below decks as a security precaution. The ships now headed into the Mediterranean and, once out of sight of land, turned westwards towards Bomba. The plan was to arrive here sometime after midnight on the 28th/29th, using a pre-positioned submarine to guide the ships in. That same night, however, came news that Italy had declared war on Greece. There were fears that she would launch an attack not just on mainland Greece, but on Crete, which lies in a dominant position in the eastern Mediterranean, as well. Consequently, the destroyers received orders to return immediately to Alexandria and the operation had to be aborted. For No. 50 ME Commando it was a bitter blow. After their intensive training of the past two weeks they were all keyed up to the highest pitch and were confident of success. The result was an understandable lowering of morale, and considerable effort was required by the officers to restore it to its former high level. Bomba would not be the only abortive operation to be experienced by the Middle East Commandos.

In the meantime, the ME Commando expansion programme was now well under way. The remainder of No. 50 were being trained, and volunteers for two more Commandos, Nos. 51 and 52, began to be vetted. No. 52, like No. 50, was to be raised from units serving in the Middle East. However, commanding officers, especially since the war had now become more active, resented having to let go officers and men whom they could ill afford to lose, and some took the opportunity to unload their bad hats on No. 52, something which was to create problems in the context of the unique form of individual discipline which the Middle East Commandos were trying to instil in their men. No. 51 ME Commando, on the other hand, had more unusual origins.

On the outbreak of war in 1939, it had been decided to resurrect the Labour Corps of 1914–18, but under a different title, the

Auxiliary Military Pioneer Corps (AMPC). At the beginning of 1940, a further decision was taken to raise AMPC companies from the indigenous peoples of the many places in the world where British and Imperial troops were deployed. Among these areas was Palestine, and a number of such companies were raised there, the first of which was originally titled No. 1 Palestinian Company AMPC. Appointed to command this was Major H.J. Cator MC of the Royal Scots Greys. He himself was an unusual man, who had been commissioned into the Greys in 1915 and served with them on the Western Front for the remainder of the war. It was there that he won his MC and also gained his nickname 'Kid' because of his youthful appearance. He had left the Army in the early 1920s in order to help his father manage the family farm, which bordered on the Royal Estate at Sandringham in Norfolk. Through invitations to shoot at Sandringham he became a personal friend of the Royal Family. When war was declared in 1939, Cator, who was still on the Reserve of Officers, hurried north to Edinburgh to rejoin his regiment as a senior subaltern, notwithstanding the fact that, on paper at least, he was scheduled to join the 6th Royal Norfolks as major and second-in-command.

At the end of September 1939, the Greys, Kid Cator with them, sailed for Palestine, where they were to join the 1st Cavalry Division which was then being formed there. The next few months were spent in pursuing Arab dissidents – a task in which the British Army had been engaged since the outbreak of the Arab rebellion three years earlier.

As his diary intimates, Cator, although he found some kindred spirits in the regiment and had plenty of opportunity to indulge in his passion for game shooting, increasingly found himself 'a fish out of water', especially since the quartermaster was the only other officer who had served with him in France more than 20 years earlier. Therefore, when he heard that the Palestinian AMPC companies were being formed and needed British officers to command them, he jumped at the chance to volunteer, especially when he heard that some would be going to France to join the British Expeditionary Force (BEF).

On 31 January 1940, Cator took over command of No. 1 Palestinian Company AMPC, which had already been warned off for France. His first pay parade gave him the opportunity to size up his men:

A 'foreign legion' would be a more accurate way of describing them, than by calling them Palestinian Pioneers. Three quarters of them are Jews and about a quarter Arab. Poles, Czechs, Russians, Bulgarians, Roumanians, Austrians, Germans and Spaniards, even Portuguese and Latvians, amongst the Arab section, Sudanese, Egyptians, Iraqis and Sinaites and Palestinians.[2]

From the start, however, Cator was determined that there should be no segregation of any form between Jew and Arab and this was surprisingly successful. At no time was there any trouble between the two, thus demonstrating that it is possible for them to get along with one another. On 20 February, Wavell inspected the company and was clearly impressed. Two days later it set sail for France.

On arrival at Marseilles on the morning of 29 February, the company, now redesignated 401 (Palestinian) Company AMPC, entrained for Rennes, where it was to be employed on the BEF's lines of communication. When the Germans invaded on 10 May and during the next few weeks, the Palestinians found themselves as mere bystanders to the momentous events which were taking place further east. Only after the evacuation of the BEF from Dunkirk did action seem imminent and the company concentrate more seriously on weapon training and defence schemes. On 16 June, with the decision to evacuate the lines of communication elements, since plans to send another BEF to France had been abandoned, the company was moved to St Malo area. Here it helped to cover the evacuation, but Cator's hopes for action were not to be realised as the Germans did not appear.

> The last 3 and 4 days have been nothing short of a miracle as regards the Palestinians, the fact that they felt they were going to fight and get an opportunity to kill developed them into a unit whose discipline was 2nd to none. In many ways I wish they had the chance to be subjected to the 'acid test' but I am *completely* confident no Battn. of Guards would have accounted for themselves better, if the opportunity to fight had arisen.[3]

Next day they were embarked in two Brixham trawlers and were landed at Weymouth. The voyage was not without incident, however. The skipper of Cator's vessel had to be carried aboard at St Malo on a stretcher since he was paralytically drunk. Later during the night he sobered up, but became incapable once more and had to be locked in his cabin. It was left to Cator and the mate to navigate the trawler, a task not made any easier by the fact that neither knew the exact location of the minefields which had been laid off the Dorset coast and the constant fear of German aircraft putting in an appearance. Eventually, after feeling their way in opposite Lulworth Cove they managed to tack themselves onto a convoy entering Weymouth. As for the drunken skipper, Cator learnt from the mate that the captain was normally a very sober man, but his recourse to drink had been brought about by the fact that a soldier (not one of Cator's men) had smuggled his French girl friend, disguised in battledress, aboard. It was a common and strong superstition among fishermen that it was most unlucky to allow a woman aboard and take her to sea.

Immediately on his return to England, Cator began to agitate for his Palestinians to be made into a proper fighting unit. Meanwhile, the Palestinians had become split up, part were with Cator in Weymouth and then, for a few days, at Westward Ho in North Devon, while the remainder were stationed at Clacton-on-Sea. By the end of June, though, they had all been concentrated at Clacton and made responsible for a sector of the anti-invasion defences in that area. This role lasted less than two weeks, and, to Cator's annoyance, his Palestinians were now moved to Camberley, where they were employed once more on labouring tasks. Cator continued to press his case for a more combatant role, lobbying Lord Lloyd, the Secretary of State for the Colonies, and even the King and Queen, with whom he took tea one day. Finally, it transpired that the intention was to raise an Arab-Jewish brigade in the Middle East, and Cator and his men were to return there to form part of it.

By this time, the raising of the UK-based Commandos was in full swing, with nine Commandos being formed. Lord Keyes, who had just assumed as Director of Combined Operations, had passed Cator's name to MO9, the War Office branch which had been created to plan Commando operations, and he was summoned there for an interview. It was probably this that gave him the idea that his Palestinians should become a Middle East Commando, especially since it is likely that MO9 would have told him that No. 50 was in the process of being formed. As it was, this interview took place on the eve of the departure of the Palestinians for Egypt and Cator was not prepared to desert them at this late hour, even though he was doubtless flattered at the invitation to become a UK-based Commando officer.

Cator and his Palestinians set sail from Gourock on the Clyde on 6 August 1940, proceeding via Freetown and Cape Town. Thus, it was not until 15 September that they arrived at Suez. To greet them was a personal message from Wavell:

> As the first Palestinian unit to join the BEF, you all bore on your shoulders the responsibility of showing to the whole of the British Empire that Palestine was determined to play a full part in the War. You have carried out that responsibility well. I am glad to learn that you won good opinions in France so that the BEF looked forward to subsequent units arriving from Palestine.[4]

The Palestinians were put into a tented camp at Geneifa and, on 19 September, Cator heard from Wavell that some 300 of his men were to form the nucleus of three Commandos. This would be once they had had some leave. In any event, as we have seen, the equipment was not available for them to begin their training straightaway. On their return from leave, Cator set about selecting suitable Commando material. By this time it had been decided that Cator's men would form just one Commando, No. 51, and that the balance of the 600 officers and men under his command would continue as No. 1 Palestinian Company AMPC.

On 15 October 1940, No. 51 Middle East Commando officially came into being. Most of the officers and British NCOs were volunteers from units in the theatre, as was the case with No. 50. As second-in-command Cator selected a fellow cavalryman, C.D.O. Miller, known as 'Gertie', of the 10th Hussars, and, among the others, there were a number who had played first-class rugby football, including Philip Keymer and Douglas Lowe. Ian Lapraik of the Cameronians had a reputation as an athlete and would go on to have a highly distinguished career in the Special Boat Service and SAS, and Henry Frost of the Cheshires was another who showed early promise.

No. 52 ME Commando formed up two weeks later than No. 51, on 2 November. No less than 35 different cap badges were represented in its ranks and, as in No. 51, some of its officers would go on to distinguish themselves later in the war. David Smiley of the Royal Horse Guards became a leading SOE figure in Albania, while William Seymour, the adjutant, would serve with Special Forces in Burma. Many, though, as in No. 50, were later killed or captured on Crete. Many of the men, on the other hand, had long conduct sheets and it was clear that, as has been stated already, commanding officers had taken the opportunity to rid themselves of undesirables. The attempts to develop self-discipline merely served to aggravate the problem, and matters were not helped by GHQ MELF's insistence that men could only be returned to their units on the grounds of physical unfitness. Demanding training schemes did, however, enable some to be weeded out for this reason.

No. 51 ME Commando did not, in contrast, suffer from the same problem. In part this was because it was formed mainly from one unit and also because Cator himself did not hold with this type of discipline and refused to implement it.

In terms of physical endurance, both Nos. 51 and 52 carried out some impressive cross-country marches. David Smiley recalls covering 33 miles in 11 hours across the desert, while No. 51 undertook a 50-mile march through rocky and hilly jebel. The fastest time was 15¾ hours, which was achieved by Ian Lapraik's section, and even Cator himself did it in 18 hours. Philip Keymer recalled:

When the pressure came some of us started to tire, but the Arabs took their boots off and hung them round their necks to get down to serious walking. I was a bit put out when I dismissed my men at the end and they all ran off to get their meal. I gingerly walked away with very sore feet!

Keymer also refers to the physical fitness of the Arabs when it came to watermanship:

No one knew anything about rowing, except one rather light weight Arab whom we put as stroke. As soon as we started to row – I was just behind him – muscles appeared all over his back and he slaughtered us! On further enquiry it transpired that he had been a fisherman on the Sea of Galilee!

During this period plans were set in motion to enlarge the Middle East Commandos even further. Within the theatre it was proposed to raise No. 53 ME Commando, but this could not be done until more equipment had been made available. GHQ India had been approached over the plan to raise three Indian Commandos for service in the Middle East and it was suggested that they should consist of one Gurkha, one Punjabi Mussulman and one Pathan Commando. This idea foundered. The Indian Army was in the midst of an enormous expansion scheme and there was a grave shortage of British officers. GHQ India's counter-proposal that two Indian Commandos should be raised from troops already in the Middle East fell on stony ground. Another idea was to form a Commando from the Polish Brigade in the Middle East, but this was rejected by General Sikorski, who headed the Polish Government-in-Exile in London, on the grounds that Poland was not at war with Italy.

One step that was taken, however, was the organisation of a Middle East Commando depot, which would be responsible for training and supplying individual reinforcements to the three Commandos when they were in action. This came into being in mid-December 1940 and was formally established, under command of Major D.W. Melville MC, on 25 January 1941, by which time all three Commandos were deployed and it was realised that they would wither away unless trained reinforcements were available to replace battle and other casualties.

This reflected yet another difference from the UK-based Commando organisation. Not until February 1942 was a centralised training organisation, the Commando Basic Training Centre at Achnacarry, set up and it was over a year later that the Holding Operational Commando was established to provide reinforcements. Interestingly enough, the Achnacarry training course also lasted for six weeks, but there does not appear to be any evidence that this was fixed as a result of the Middle East Commando experience. Indeed, as will now have become apparent, the two Commando organisations were totally divorced from one another.

Operationally, after the abortive Bomba raid there was a lull. As the weeks passed by, it seemed that the Italians had little intention of continuing their advance towards the Suez Canal and Wavell decided that the time had come to take offensive action against them. Plans were therefore drawn up for what became known as Operation *Compass*. In East Africa, too, he decided that steps must be taken to clear the Italian presence. To do this, he planned a pincer movement, with General Platt advancing from the north and General Cunningham coming up from Kenya in the south.

Before this could happen, though, Platt had to eradicate the Italian lodgements in Sudan. In early November 1940 troops of General Heath's 5th Indian Division launched attacks towards Kassala and Gallabat, but both were blocked and there was now another pause until the new year while further supplies were brought up. In the Mediterranean, the Fleet Air Arm mounted a highly successful attack on the Italian Fleet in Taranto harbour, but on 28 October Mussolini had launched an invasion of Greece through Albania. It was this which prompted the next operational deployment for the Middle East Commandos.

At the beginning of the war it had been agreed that Crete, with its vital strategic position in the eastern Mediterranean, should be a French responsibility, especially since the Greek Government would not countenance the stationing of British forces there. The French capitulation and now the Italian invasion of Greece from Albania changed this situation and the British took immediate steps to occupy the island. Of especial importance was Suda Bay, on the north coast of the island, which was an ideal fleet anchorage and a perfect advanced base for the Mediterranean Fleet.

On 5 November 1940, one troop of No. 50 Commando, that which had been used in the Bomba operation, sailed for Crete as part of *Assumption* Force, which was built round Brigadier O.H. Tidbury's 14 Infantry Brigade. Two weeks later, the remainder of the Commando, which had now completed its training, received similar orders and was issued with battledress, the first time that many of its members who had spent time in the Middle East had seen it.

Before they left, however, there was a change in commanding officer. Harry Fox-Davies had earlier been posted across to take command of No. 52, his place as second-in-command being taken by Stephen Rose. Now he fell sick and, in view of No. 52's domestic problems over discipline, it was decided that George Young should move across and take temporary command of them. As it happened, Fox-Davies's illness proved more serious than was first thought and he had to be medically downgraded, and George Young was appointed to the permanent command of No. 52. Fox-Davies did, however, recover and rejoined his regiment, winning a Military Cross in the spring of 1941. He then achieved his ambition of serving in action with Special Forces, joining the Long Range Desert Group, but tragically was killed on his first patrol. In George Young's place in No. 50 ME Commando came Lt-Colonel Peter Symons, who had been an infantryman during the First World War, but had now been recalled as a Royal Engineer on the grounds that he had done some copper mining between the wars.

The move of the balance of No. 50 to Crete coincided with a decision to temporarily redeploy the Mediterranean Fleet from Alexandria to Malta. Thus, the commandos were privileged enough to find themselves as passengers in the battleships *Warspite, Valiant* and the cruiser *York*. Sir Andrew Cunningham, the Commander-in-Chief, was flying in his flag in the *Warspite* and showed particular interest in the Commando, closely questioning Stephen Rose on its organisation and role. Although the Commandos themselves did not know it at the time, Cunningham had written to the First Sea Lord, Sir Dudley Pound, on 21 November suggesting that 'perhaps the Dodecanese were ripe for plucking and that General Wavell had a commando type unit which was to be based on Crete'.[5] On 26 November they arrived at Suda Bay, having been attacked by high flying Italian aircraft, which luckily scored no hits, as they passed through the Kaso Straits separating the eastern tip of Crete from the island of Kasos. Having disembarked, the commandos were told that they were to be deployed to Heraklion, 80 miles to the east of Suda Bay, and that same day they took passage in a Fleet Auxiliary, the *Fiona*. This proved to be a somewhat uncomfortable voyage. *Fiona* was carrying a cargo of bombs and fuel for the RAF and many of the flimsy petrol tins (this was before the days of the jerrican) stowed on the deck were leaking. It would only have taken one enemy incendiary round or carelessness by the crew or troops on board for disaster to happen. Nevertheless, it proved to be an uninterrupted passage and on arrival the commandos were greeted by Captain John Pendlebury, the British Vice-Consul at Heraklion.

Pendlebury was to become a very good friend of No. 50 ME Commando and was in many ways an unusual man. While up at Cambridge in the 1920s, he had made a name for himself as a high jumper and hurdler and was a contemporary of those two legendary athletes of the era, H.W. Abrahams and Lord Burleigh. He was also a good cricketer, and all this with only one eye, having lost the other in a childhood accident. On coming down from Cambridge in 1927, his heart was set on becoming an archaeologist and he later went to Crete, becoming curator of Knossos during 1930–35 and writing the Knossos Handbook. After giving up the curatorship, he remained in Crete, carrying out further archaeological work, until the eve of war in 1939, when he returned to England. Here he managed to obtain a commission in a cavalry regiment. In May 1940, however, he was ordered to report to the War Office, MI(R) Branch to be exact. His singular knowledge of Greece, and especially Crete, had been remembered.

In the company of Nicholas Hammond, who was to become one of the SOE stars in the Balkans, and others, Pendlebury was sent to Greece on the assumption that Italy would soon be in the war and that she might well turn her eyes towards the Balkans. If this should happen, there was a need for officers on the ground to organise guerrilla and partisan warfare. They were to be controlled by Adrian Simpson and MI(R) Branch in Cairo. The Greeks, however, were very suspicious of the party on its arrival and refused some members, including Hammond, permission to stay and they were forced to go on to Egypt. Pendlebury, on the other hand, did manage to get himself back to Crete and was beginning to organise a guerrilla infrastructure there when No. 50 ME Commando arrived.

Pendlebury found No. 50 good quarters, partly in a school and tobacco factory, with the remainder being allocated part of the barracks on the airfield, and the welcome from the locals, now that Italy had attacked Greece, was especially warm. The local Cretan division had been sent to fight in Albania and in its place troops from the mainland had been sent to the island. They viewed the arrival of the British troops with much suspicion, possibly because they feared that they might encourage self-government for the island. There were also a number of people there who were either German, and it must be remembered that Germany was not yet at war with Greece, or had definite sympathies in this direction. In particular, among the Germans was one of the leading surgeons in the local hospital at Heraklion, who evinced great friendliness towards the Commando and saved one of the men's lives after he had been accidentally shot in the stomach and bowel. There was also the secretary to the British Consul in Heraklion, a certain bearded Herr Rosenbusch, and the lighthouse keeper at Cape Sidero, which overlooked the Kaso Straits and the sea route taken by the Royal Navy's ships arriving from Alexandria, was known to be sympathetic to the Axis. Thus, operational security was always a very real problem. But this was not the only difficulty which No. 50 faced.

The headquarters of 14 Infantry Brigade, under whose command No. 50 now was, was 80 miles away at Canea. The only transport which the Commando had was one staff car, one three-ton and one 15 cwt truck and hence communication was always difficult. The fact, too, that embarkation for operations took place on the harbour quay, which was overlooked by the town of Heraklion, and the troops had to march down to the harbour, because of the transport shortage, meant that the locals knew when an operation was being mounted, which did not help security.

Apart from being given a sector of the island to defend against Italian sabotage parties, it soon became clear that Cunningham was keen that the commandos on Crete should be used in their proper role of amphibious raids, and efforts were made to train for these. Unfortunately, there were still no powered landing craft available in the Mediterranean and on Crete there were not even any spare naval whalers. Thus No. 50 had to make do with locally requisitioned craft, many of which were unseaworthy and required extensive repairs in order to make them usable. Nevertheless, a drill was devised whereby some 60 men could be landed simultaneously using a diesel-engined caique towing two 'strings' of local boats. All very primitive, but it was something. One compensation was, however, that as far as realistic training was concerned there were good opportunities to exercise over rough terrain with live ammunition. Thus, by the end of 1940, No. 50 ME Commando was poised for offensive operations and merely awaiting specific orders. Meanwhile the other two Middle East Commandos had not been idle.

CHAPTER TWO

Compass and Castelorizzo

On 28 November 1940, both Nos. 51 and 52 Middle East
Commandos were put on 24 hours' notice to move from 1 December.
The reason for this was *Compass*, which was due to be launched on the
9th. Initially it was to be merely a three-day operation against the
fortified Italian camps in Egypt, but Adrian Simpson hoped that the
Commandos might be found a role in the plan. The warning order
for No. 52 was, however, cancelled on 1 December and instead
George Young was warned that he must be prepared to move to the
Sudan any time after the 15th.

No. 51, on the other hand, was quickly given a task in connection
with *Compass*. On 3 December, Kid Cator was summoned to GHQ
MELF to see General (later Field Marshal The Lord) 'Jumbo'
Wilson, GOC British Troops Egypt, and briefed on what was
required of him. The idea was to land three parties, each of 20 men,
near Buq Buq, some 25 miles behind the Italian front line, and cut
the water pipeline which ran from Capuzzo to Sidi Barrani. Cator
selected four officers, one warrant officer and 38 Raiders and the
party was, on 7 December, ordered aboard HMS *Medway*, the
submarine depot ship for the Mediterranean Fleet. Next day, Cator
attended a conference held in the *Warspite*, where he learnt that his
party was to be embarked in *Hereward*, which had taken part in No.
50's abortive raid on Bomba.

Cator now briefed his men, and later issued his officers with fish
hooks and line. These, he said, were to put through the ears of
prisoners to prevent them from escaping. His officers were somewhat
taken aback by this rather barbaric means of securing prisoners and,
as Philip Keymer recalled: 'None of us had the slightest intention of
using them.' Indeed, many of his officers thought him slightly
eccentric, especially in his fetish for physical fitness, which included
boxing three rounds before breakfast with any luckless officer or
NCO whom he could compel to join him. Nevertheless, there is no
doubt that he more than retained the loyalty of his Palestinians.

On the 9th, the day that *Compass* was launched with such success,
Cator and his men embarked in *Hereward* (Lt-Commander Greening
RN) and steamed out of Alexandria at 0600 hours the following

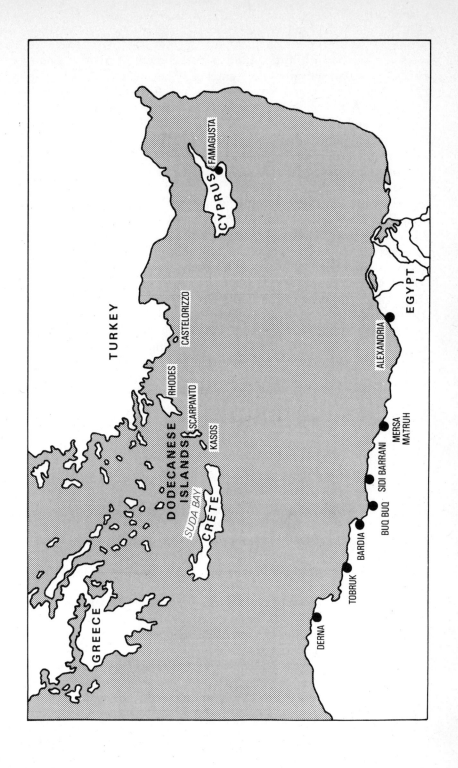

TURKEY

GREECE

CYPRUS

FAMAGUSTA

EGYPT

ALEXANDRIA

CASTELORIZZO

RHODES

DODECANESE ISLANDS

SCARPANTO

KASOS

SUDA BAY

CRETE

MERSA MATRUH

SIDI BARRANI

BUQ BUQ

BARDIA

TOBRUK

DERNA

morning. In the meantime, another detachment of 64 men under Henry Frost had set sail in the lighter *X.39*, a veteran of Gallipoli in 1915. The skipper of this vessel was a colourful character, Lieutenant A.B. Palmer RNR, known universally as 'Pedlar'. Born in Australia he had first gone to sea in 1916 on board a sailing vessel bound for England, only to be sunk by a U-boat off Land's End and subsequently to survive two and a half days in an open lifeboat before reaching Penzance in Cornwall. He then enlisted in the Royal Navy and served with the Grand Fleet. Between the wars he continued to be wed to the sea, spending much time based at Shanghai, where he joined the US National Guard contingent. Recalled to active duty in 1939 he eventually found himself posted to HMS *Medway*. Now his task was to steam up the coast and land ammunition and supplies for 7th Armoured Division beyond Sidi Barrani.

The sea was very rough when *Hereward* set sail, but even so she kept up a speed of 20 knots and arrived off Sollum Bay at 2100 hours. By this time, most of the commandos had succumbed to seasickness, although not Cator. He was determined to go ahead with the landing, using the few men who were still fit, but Commander Greening considered that the seas were too rough to launch the whalers, in spite of Cator's attempts to persuade him otherwise. Thus the operation, which had been codenamed *Cator*, had to be aborted.

For the rest of the night *Hereward* cruised about the bay in the company of the destroyers *Nubian, Jarvis* and *Janus*. The heavy sea continued to run next day, but there was some consolation to be had in watching the old monitor HMS *Terror*, with her two 15-inch guns, bombarding Sollum and the Halfaya Pass together with the gunboats *Aphis* and *Ladybird*, which would later become well known to No. 50 ME Commando. It was hoped to try and land the commandos again that night, but once more the seas proved too rough. Instead the destroyers bombarded Sollum and received some Italian fire in return. They then returned to Alexandria, where Cator and Greening were interviewed by Cunningham, who was clearly as disappointed as they were that *Cator* had been foiled by the weather. None the less, Cator was ordered to remain on instant stand-by and it seemed that another operation could well be in the offing.

Compass had gone better than anyone could have possibly hoped. The measure of surprise achieved and the fact that the fortified camps were not positioned so as to be able to provide mutual support meant that they were quickly overrun and the Italians, apart from their garrisons at Sollum and Sidi Omar, driven back into Libya.

Wavell and O'Connor, commanding the Western Desert Force, were now thinking of capitalising on their success rather than close the operation down. Meanwhile, Cator and his men remained on board *Medway* awaiting their next summons.

On the 17th, Sidi Omar and Sollum fell and eyes were now turned on the stronghold of Bardia. Next day, Cator was ordered to report to HMS *Barham*, which was deputising as flagship since the bulk of the fleet was at sea. He was told that he was to embark his men in an Australian destroyer, HMAS *Voyager* (Lt-Commander Morrow RAN) and sail that night for Sollum. There he was to report to Brigadier Galloway, the Brigadier General Staff Western Desert Force, having first collected Henry Frost and his party and a company of the 3rd Coldstream Guards from Mersa Matruh. His likely objective was Bardia.

After a calm voyage, Mersa Matruh was reached at 0700 hours and Frost and the Coldstream taken on board. Continuing on to Sollum, *Voyager* struck a stiff breeze which caused a further bout of seasickness, although it was the Coldstream who suffered most. Arriving at Sollum at 1230 hours, Cator was briefed by Galloway.

The plan was that the commandos should transship to *Aphis*, while the Coldstream went on board *Ladybird*. No. 51 would then land at Bardia with the Coldstream in support. Prospects looked especially good when the captain of the *Aphis*, Lt-Commander Campbell, told how he had taken his ship into Bardia that very morning and subjected it to a bombardment which had created wholesale panic, with much waving of white handkerchiefs, tablecloths and other items.

Yet, once more frustration set in. Apparently the leading elements of the Western Desert Force had given their position as being 6,000 yards further west than it actually was, and instead of being at the perimeter of the Bardia defences they were some distance from it. A landing was therefore considered too risky and the operation was postponed. Brigadier Galloway ordered the Coldstream back to Mersa Mutruh and Cator was told to assume command at Sollum.

In the meantime, *X.39* was sunk in an air raid on Mersa Matruh and Palmer was eventually given command of a captured Italian schooner. He spent much of 1941 running the blockade of Tobruk to bring in supplies to the beleaguered garrison, but his luck ran out after an engine failure and he was captured. Later he was to lose an arm during an escape attempt and was repatriated. He won a DSC and was made an MBE for his war services and is still very much alive and kicking today.

Cator and his men were to remain at Sollum for the next three weeks. Their main task was to provide working parties to unload ships in the harbour. There were frequent air raids and Sollum was also bothered by an Italian 150mm gun, nicknamed Bardia Bill by the troops. Cator, however, was lucky enough to be able to accommodate his men in caves, which were proof against bombs and shells, but working conditions in the harbour were often unpleasant.

In spite of these labouring duties, which must have convinced some of the Palestinians that they were back in the AMPC, there were opportunities to carry out landing exercises, using *Aphis*, which had remained at Sollum, and other tactical schemes. Cator himself put up a proposal for another operation. This was for a landing at Appollonia, 60 miles west of Bardia. There was an Italian fighter base here, from which escorts were provided for the bombers regularly attacking Sollum. He had the idea of flying two of the aircraft back, two RAF pilots being included in the raiding party, and destroying the rest on the ground. In this instance, Cunningham did not have a destroyer to spare and so the idea was stillborn.

Another glimmer of hope was raised on 30 December when Cator had lunch with General O'Connor. By this stage 6th Australian Division was in the process of relieving 4th Indian in the line and O'Connor intended to use it to capture Bardia, whose greatest obstacle was the anti-tank ditch which had been dug around it. He was perhaps more concerned about the Australians' reputation for indiscriminate looting and wanted to use No. 51 ME Commando to go in with the leading troops and secure the wireless station and two or three other important buildings.

Major-General Mackay, the Australian divisional commander, would not, however, countenance the use of British troops since he wanted, perhaps understandably, the capture of Bardia to be wholly an Australian victory, although of necessity he was forced to rely on British armour, notably the Matilda tanks of 7th Royal Tank Regiment.

Thus, once again, No. 51 was frustrated and it was decided that Cator and his men should return to Geneifa. They left Sollum by road on 5 January, the day on which Bardia fell, stayed for a few days at Mersa Matruh, and were back in Geneifa by the 14th. On his return, Kid Cator submitted a diary of events for the period 7 December–12 January to Wavell and received a reply from General Arthur Smith, the Deputy Chief of Staff:

The Commander-in-Chief wishes me to tell you how much he regrets that you never had the opportunity of undertaking an operation, but he much appreciates the fine spirit which so obviously exists in No. 51 Middle East Commando and wishes the men to be so informed. Tell them that General Wavell hopes that an opportunity will soon come when they may show their fighting qualities.[1]

That opportunity, as we shall see in the next chapter, was not to be long in coming.

While No. 51 was temporarily stood down from operations, north across the Mediterranean on Crete No. 50 ME Commando now entered a phase of more active participation in the war. The early Commando raids on the coasts of occupied Europe which had been mounted from England in summer 1940 had not been a success and indeed had turned Churchill against the concept of small pinprick raids. Instead, he wanted larger scale operations involving 5,000 to 10,000 men.

Admiral Sir Roger Keyes, who had been appointed by Churchill as Director of Combined Operations (DCO) in July 1940, realised that such operations were not yet feasible against the Channel and North Sea enemy-held coastlines and turned his eyes to the Mediterranean. At the end of October 1940 he proposed to the Chiefs of Staff that Pantellaria, a small island lying between Sicily and the North African coast, should be attacked and captured. This would have the benefits of providing an alternative naval base to Malta and could be used to launch air attacks against the Italian lines of communication across the Mediterranean. This plan was codenamed *Workshop* and, after some hesitation, the Chiefs of Staff accepted it, provided that it did not interfere with another operation, *Brisk*, which was the seizure of the Azores should Spain enter the war on the Axis side.

Cunningham, however, was not happy about *Workshop*. He saw it as inflicting an intolerable burden on his already overstretched naval resources, especially since, once captured, the island would have to be held and supplied. Instead, he believed that more mileage was to be gained in operations against the Dodecanese, which were codenamed *Mandibles*, and this was especially so with the arrival of No. 50 ME Commando on Crete.

Nevertheless, Churchill himself preferred *Workshop*, and his belief in it was reinforced by Wavell's success against the Italians in the Western Desert. Accordingly, Keyes gathered up a force of UK Commandos (Nos. 7, 8 and 11) under Lt-Colonel Bob Laycock. The intention was to send it to the Mediterranean in three specially adapted amphibious landing ships, the Glens (*Glenearn, Glengyle* and *Glenroy*). The sailing of Force Z, as it was called, was delayed, however, by fears of a German invasion of Spain.

In the meantime, Cunningham continued to press the case for *Mandibles* and that for *Workshop* became considerably weakened in early January 1941 when the Luftwaffe began to occupy bases in Sicily in preparation for the move of German troops to Libya in order to bolster up their ally. Yet, Churchill continued to cling tenaciously to *Workshop*, but, in spite of this, Cunningham was determined to press ahead. As a first step he saw it as necessary to secure the Kaso Straits by seizing the island of Kasos and then installing coastal guns manned by Royal Marines on it in order to dominate the airfield on the neighbouring and larger island of Scarpanto. Accordingly, in early January, No. 50 ME Commando was alerted for a raid on Kasos and two Royal Navy liaison officers, Commander Nicholl, who had the distinguishing feature of a sliced-off ear, and Lieutenant McFie, were permanently attached to the Commando, an indication that it was now more the servant of the Royal Navy than the Army.

The operation was to be mounted on the night of 16/17 January 1941. Its purpose was no more than a reconnaissance of the south coast of the island in order to find a suitable landing beach and exits up the steep cliffs which abutted the shore. Indeed, given that the locally requisitioned boats were wholly unsuited to the landing of stores and ammunition, it would have been very difficult to sustain the commandos once ashore if the aim had been to capture the island. A further problem was the warship which the Royal Navy had provided for the raid. HMS *Derby* was an ancient coal-burning sloop/minesweeper of 1915 vintage. She was noisy and dirty and showers of sparks poured from her funnel whenever the boilers were stoked – hardly the most suitable craft for clandestine operations by night. Even worse, she had metal decks, no means of lowering extra boats and lacked scrambling nets. About all that could be said in her favour was her shallow draught which provided some reassurance when cruising along the coast in uncertain waters.

The operation was mounted as planned and *Derby* succeeded in making landfall. With the aid of improvised davits, the commandos were transferred to their motley collection of small craft. Many of these sprang leaks, caused by the rough handling they received while being lowered into the water, and one or two even sank. At this moment a signal was received ordering the cancellation of the operation, and the expedition had to extricate itself and return to Crete.

The decision to cancel was not because of the problems being experienced in landing or even that Cunningham had changed his mind. In London no decision had yet been made as to whether Z Force, which was still in Scotland, should be used for *Workshop* or *Mandibles*, and it was considered that in the meantime nothing was to be gained by stirring up the Italians through pinprick raids in the Dodecanese. At the end of January 1941, Churchill and the Chiefs of Staff finally reached agreement that *Mandibles* rather than *Workshop* should be pursued, and on the last day of the month Z Force set sail from the Isle of Arran for the Mediterranean, using the Cape route. The ultimate objective of *Mandibles* was to be the capture of Rhodes (codename *Cordite*), and in early February Cunningham was given permission to resume his operations against the smaller Dodecanese islands provided that these fitted into the overall plan. Consequently, the Kasos operation (*Blunt*) was resurrected once more.

In view of the abortive operation in January, it was decided that another reconnaissance of the island was needed before the attack itself was mounted. This time the north coast was selected. In order to improve landing techniques, No. 50 was allowed to use *Derby* for practices in Sitia Bay, which is situated in the north-east corner of Crete.

At this juncture, John Pendlebury stepped in and said that he knew of Greek guides on the island and it was agreed that he and a fellow SOE member and archaeologist, Jack Hamson, should accompany the party from No. 50 in order to contact them in person. The second attempt on Kasos was mounted on the night of 17/18 February and was even more abortive than the first. For a start, faulty navigation and mistakes over the time and tides meant that the party was landed on the wrong beach. Not surprisingly, Pendlebury was unable to locate his guides, let alone the beach exits for which he was looking. There was therefore no option but to return to the ship. The late Colonel Michael Borwick, who took part as a member of No. 50, remembered:

> The captain of HMS *Derby* had a very unpleasant bull terrier which bit me in the backside and started to bark its head off just as Commander Nicholl was returning from a reconnaissance. The clouds rolled away and there was a large gun emplacement waiting for the unwary. The Royal Italian flag was hoisted by the *Derby* as a *ruse de guerre* and we sailed away to Crete.

Another disappointment, but Cunningham was in no way

disheartened. His eyes merely turned from the western to the eastern end of the Dodecanese.

The island of Castelorizzo (*Pitch*) is the most easterly of the Dodecanese, lying some 80 miles from Rhodes and, significantly, just three miles from the Turkish coast. It had a number of attractions as a target in Cunningham's eyes. Since it was out on a limb, he did not believe, mistakenly as it turned out, that the enemy could quickly launch a counter-attack if it was captured. It would also be most useful as a motor torpedo boat base in support of subsequent operations in the Dodecanese.

Finally, and on the larger canvas, there was the effect that its capture might have on Turkey's attitude to the war. A military mission had been sent to Ankara under General Sir James Marshall-Cornwall in December 1940 in order to persuade the Turks to come into the war on the British side. This was to be followed up at the end of February 1941 by a visit by Anthony Eden, the Foreign Secretary, and General Sir John Dill, Chief of the Imperial General Staff, both to Athens, in order to reassure the Greeks of British support in the event of a German invasion and damp down jealousy brought about by the wooing of Turkey, and to Ankara, as reinforcement to General Marshall-Cornwall's efforts. If Castelorizzo, on Turkey's doorstep, could be seized and secured while this visit was taking place, there was no saying what a favourable influence this might have on the Turks.

Cunningham entrusted the planning of Operation *Abstention*, as it was dubbed, to Rear Admiral E. de F. Renouf, Flag Officer 3rd Cruiser Squadron. Time, however, was very short and Admiral Renouf himself did not arrive with his squadron in Suda Bay until the day before the force had to sail. His plan was for No. 50 ME Commando to be landed from the destroyers *Decoy* and *Hereward* in order to seize the island. They would then be relieved after 24 hours by a permanent garrison made up of 1st Battalion The Sherwood Foresters, who were then in Cyprus. No air support could be made available by day, but the RAF agreed to bomb the airfield on Rhodes during the nights of 25/26 and 26/27 February when the operation was at its height. In the event, this never took place since priority was given to the protection of a convoy bound for Malta.

There was very little available in the way of intelligence and what there was came mainly from French sources, gathered when Air France had used Castelorizzo harbour as a seaplane base in the mid-1930s. Otherwise there was just one Italian chart and some picture postcards and there was very little information on the size of the garrison. Because of this, Renouf decided that the landing must take place during the hours of darkness and selected Niftis Point, east of Castelorizzo harbour, as the point of landing.

No. 50 ME Commando had by now a laid-down drill for preparing for amphibious operations. All material was broken down into easily handled loads, wrapped in blankets, to reduce the noise factor, and waterproofed. Likewise, oars were also muffled. Each man was also issued with sufficient morphine to knock himself or a comrade out. This was important. With only a doctor and three medical orderlies attached, medical support was slim and the very nature of Commando operations meant that the normal lines of communication chain on the conventional battlefield – Advanced Dressing Station, Casualty Clearing Station etc., etc. – were simply not available. Indeed, there is no doubt that commando soldiers did die on operations from wounds from which they would have recovered in a more conventional situation. This was part of the risk factor in being a commando and the men were well aware of it when the morphine issue took place.

The commandos were embarked on the evening of the 23rd and the destroyers sailed in the early hours of the following morning. This time, in order to ensure that the navigational errors which had so marred the second attempt on Kasos were not repeated, the submarine HMS *Parthian* was sent ahead to provide a navigation 'beacon'. At 0200 hours on the 25th her leading light was spotted and *Decoy* and *Hereward* steamed slowly towards Niftis Point. Two hundred yards offshore the engines were stopped and the business of transferring to the whalers began.

Each destroyer had five whalers, its normal complement of three and two additional. Any more than this would have seriously affected the efficiency of the ship in action. It meant, however, that the commandos had to be landed in two waves, and unfortunately many of the first wave became disoriented in the pitch darkness. Some overshot the Point and carried on towards the harbour, where they were challenged and came under fire. They therefore beat a hasty retreat and returned to the ships. The remainder did land in the right place and, led by Captain Borwick, quickly overcame an Italian patrol with Tommy gun fire and pressed on towards the town and harbour.

By now, dawn was not far off and Commander E.G. McGregor DSO RN, captain of the *Decoy* and the senior naval officer, was becoming increasingly concerned since he had strict orders to be clear of the island by daylight. The fact, though, that some commandos had been successfully landed persuaded him to continue the operation and eventually all were put safely ashore. The destroyers now departed to join the rest of 3rd Cruiser Squadron at Cyprus for their next task, the escorting of the Foresters to Castelorizzo, but left the gunboat *Ladybird* behind to give fire support to the commandos.

The key objective on the island was Paleocastro Fort in the centre, which stood atop rocky slopes rising some 800 feet from the harbour, and it was now that *Ladybird* began to show her worth. As the commandos scrambled up towards the fort, so she pumped twelve 6-inch shells into it. The garrison, numbering some 50 men, immediately surrendered to the commandos as they reached the crest. But, with the arrival of daylight, the Italian Air Force became active and a penalty had to be paid for not suppressing the Rhodes airfield. Savoia 81 three-engined bombers, escorted by Caproni 42 fighters, appeared overhead and life became very unpleasant.

An early casualty was *Ladybird* who was hit by a bomb on one of her turrets, wounding all the gun crew, some seriously. It was clearly too much of a risk to leave her exposed like this and hence she departed for Cyprus and had to fight off several air attacks while on passage. Nevertheless, the commandos themselves managed to account for three enemy aircraft and, furthermore, had secured the island well before midday. The Union Flag was run up on the Customs House, which was situated at the entrance of the harbour, the Italian Governor had been made prisoner and high-grade cipher books obtained from his safe.

The rest of the day was spent in organising the defence of the island, but intermittent air attacks continued until dusk. By this time, all ranks of No. 50 were very tired after 36 hours with virtually no sleep. Thus, after posting sentries, the remainder settled down for some urgently needed rest, confident that the morrow would see the arrival of the Foresters.

Suddenly, at about 2100 hours, the harbour was lit up by a searchlight. Next moment, two Italian L Class torpedo boats, accompanied by E-boats, appeared, firing for all they were worth. This was totally unexpected, since it had been assumed that the Royal Navy would ensure that enemy shipping was kept away from the island. In the resultant confusion, the Italian craft succeeded in rescuing a number of Italians who had earlier sought refuge in the waterfront houses and were gone as suddenly as they came. The commandos consequently spent the rest of the night on stand to in case there was a repeat performance.

What concerned Symons now was that the relief force, which was due to arrive shortly, should be warned of what had happened. Indeed, the Foresters were on their way, albeit with only a company in the armed boarding vessel *Rosaura* rather than the complete battalion which No. 50 had been led to expect, and *Hereward* had been sent on ahead.

Unfortunately, wireless communications were at the best imperfect. The commandos had one wireless set only, with a range of just 50 miles and not in proper working order. Thus, the only way in which the defenders on shore could effectively communicate with the ships was by light signal, but this was dependent on the ship being close enough to the shore to be able to see it. As it was, *Hereward* arrived off the coast at 2300 hours and received a garbled message that enemy surface craft were in the area and could possibly be about to attempt a landing. She therefore passed an 'enemy sighted' report to Renouf but, instead of remaining in the area to check this out and give assistance to the commandos if need be, she returned to the squadron.

Renouf considered that it was now much too risky to try and land the Foresters, especially since there were not sufficient hours of darkness left. In addition, the destroyers were now running short of fuel. He therefore decided to take the complete squadron back to Alexandria to refuel and then make another attempt, but there was no way in which the commandos could be informed of this. This meant that No. 50 ME Commando was to be left isolated on Castelorizzo in a totally hostile air and sea environment for the next 48 hours and in complete ignorance of Renouf's amended plan.

During the 26th, air attacks continued intermittently all day, although not with quite the same intensity as the day before. The commandos did their best to restore some semblance of order on the island, but this was not made easy when the Greek islanders' celebrations over the defeat of the Italians got somewhat out of hand. All Italian-owned houses were looted and there were squabbles over the ownership of boats in the harbour. Nevertheless, the belief that they would be relieved that night kept morale well up, although in truth Renouf's ships only arrived at Alexandria at 2000 hours. It is highly probable that the Italians were aware of this from reconnaissance aircraft and knew that they had plenty of time in which to mount an operation to recapture the island. It was only two hours' steaming time from Rhodes, but at least twelve from Alexandria.

Consequently, at 1030 hours on the 27th, two torpedo boats, again accompanied by E-boats, once more arrived in the harbour. Supported by naval bombardment and air strikes, some 200 marines and Alpini artillery were quickly landed from a small transport. Armed with nothing heavier than Bren guns, there was nothing that the commandos could do about this and they were soon forced to give up the low ground, since they did not have the men to cover it, and withdrew to higher ground from which they could not be overlooked. Ammunition was running low, food and, especially water, were short and casualties were mounting. The situation looked grim.

In the meantime, at Alexandria the Foresters had been transferred to *Decoy* and *Hero*, which had taken *Hereward*'s place, much to the annoyance of the latter's crew who had built up a close rapport with the commandos. Having refuelled, the ships weighed anchor at 0710 hours on 27 February, but would not arrive off Castelorizzo until 2315 hours that night. During this time No. 50 had been gradually forced back to a small area on the south side of the island which had a small path leading down to a beach below the high cliffs. A.C. Darby:

> When darkness fell that night I was given a small number of men to form a buffer between the enemy and our own defensive position and I spread my men out at regular intervals about 200 yards in front of our lines having begged as many grenades and as much ammo as could be spared. By that time we were very short of ammo and damned hungry. During that dark period of loneliness – we were spread very thin on the ground – I wriggled forward some way until I could hear muted enemy voices and, having decided that there was no future in hanging around at that point, withdrew to my small 'buffer'. Not a very constructive action on my part but at least I knew the exact location of some of the opposition. Shortly afterwards one of my group reported signals from the sea and I sent back a runner with the information, but I believe our HQ had already made contact with our own ships carrying the Sherwood Foresters – three days late.

Once *Decoy* and *Hero* had hove to off the coast of Castelorizzo, Major Cooper and some 50 men of the Foresters were landed by boat, together with their kitbags and packs, in order to establish what was happening. While this was taking place, the Commandos managed to establish communications with *Decoy* using matches and an electric torch. Lieutenant (later Brigadier) Michael Blackman was commanding one of the Foresters' platoons which went ashore:

> The whalers from *Decoy* put us ashore at dead of night at exactly the right place and at the right time. I was commanding the leading platoon and I

and my naval signaller quickly scrambled over the half submerged rocks and up to the hillside track leading to the one and only township on the island. But it was then that my elan became somewhat blunted.

The first evidence of the ME Commando presence that the Foresters came across was an abandoned stone breastwork, and then the body of a British soldier. A little further on they met two commandos who had been cut off during the withdrawal to the high ground and were intending to swim to Turkey. As a result of their account, Major Cooper realised that all was not well and signalled *Decoy* that he was coming aboard once more in order to decide what should be done.

From his information and what the commandos had been able to indicate by torch, it was quite clear that the island was now untenable and the decision was taken to re-embark the whole force. With some difficulty, in view of the darkness and steadily rising sea, the commandos and Foresters were successfully taken on board, and the force sailed for Crete, where the survivors of No. 50 were disembarked. 3rd Cruiser Squadron, with the Foresters still on board, then returned to Alexandria.

It was inevitable that some of the Middle East commandos were cut off and could not be evacuated. Of these, a number, like the two whom the Foresters met, decided to swim for the Turkish coast. One of these was Lance-Corporal Dick Sheehy of the Warwickshire Yeomanry, but he was captured before he could reach the seashore.

> The troops who took us were Black Shirt fascists who were quite nasty. We had our thumbs tied together with cord behind our backs and were then booted and bayoneted in the buttocks all the way up the saddle to our old Commando position. The next hour or so was not very amusing either, but as the party was getting rough, the Italian admiral and staff from Rhodes, who were having a look round, rescued us with much talk of the Geneva Convention etc. We were taken to the harbour side and shut in an ammunition magazine where a lot of Sherwood Foresters packs had been dumped, presumably by the Ities. Our captors gave us a couple of Sherwood greatcoats and some tobacco and cigarettes from the same source.

A few days later they were flown across to Rhodes in a seaplane, being tied to the aircraft stanchions by their thumbs. There Sheehy and his compatriot were placed in a temporary prison and reunited with eleven other members of No. 50. There were also a number of Greeks from Castelorizzo here and these were badly beaten up and 'some we suspected were killed'. They were also bothered by

Luftwaffe pilots who seemed to delight in taking photographs of them. They were then taken by corvette to Taranto, where the sight of the sunken Italian warships, victims of the Fleet Air Arm attack in November 1940, did much to raise morale. It was in Taranto that Dick Sheehy and his comrades began to adapt to the POW existence which was to be their lot for the next four years.

Some attempted the swim to Turkey, but drowned. Others were more fortunate, including Trooper Len Addicott, also a Warwickshire Yeoman. He succeeded in reaching the Turkish coast, although he was only semi-conscious from exhaustion by the time he beached.

> The next thing that roused me was a voice hissing in my ear 'Inglese?' and I was staring into two brown faces leaning over the gunwhale of a boat with a rifle pointed at me. Without hesitation I mouthed 'Aiwa anna Inglese'. Their faces broke into a grin and they dragged me on board. My bit of Arabic seemed to have satisfied them.

Shortly after being landed, he was, much to his surprise, greeted by two other members of No. 50, both dressed in Turkish uniform, and was taken to the local barracks, where he was similarly attired. After a few days' recuperation, all three were taken on horseback through the Taurus Mountains and thence by British Embassy car to Ankara. Here they were looked after by the embassy, but allowed to explore the capital, arousing intense but friendly interest among the populace. After a few days there they were given passports and train tickets for the port of Mersin. From here they embarked for Famagusta in Cyprus in a boat filled with Polish refugees and were back in Egypt by the end of March.

In spite of the warm welcome that the Turks gave Len Addicott and his friends, there is no doubt that the failure of *Abstention* did not help the campaign to persuade Turkey to join the war against the Axis powers, although it is only fair to mention that General Marshall-Cornwall was warning the British Government that the Turkish forces were in no state to stand up to a German attack unless they were extensively re-equipped. Clearly something had gone very wrong and it said little for Britain's future prospects in the Mediterranean. The question now was how the damage should be repaired.

Cunningham's view was that the operation should be treated, for public consumption at least, as a mere raid.[2] Harold Nicolson, however, who was Secretary of State in the Ministry of Information, recorded in his diary for 1 March 1941:

We have a row in the Duty Room with General Tripp, who represents the Admiralty on the subject of the Castelorizzo communique. We point out that our objectives were to occupy the island and that, as we were turned out by troops brought in from Rhodes, we failed to carry out our objectives. Why, therefore should they pretend that we had succeeded? We are the department charged with Government publicity and our policy is to tell the truth. If other departments without our consent put out untrue statements, our work becomes impossible. I am angry about all this.[3]

He was not the only one. A few days later Churchill addressed a minute to General Ismay:

I am thoroughly mystified about this Operation, and I think it is the duty of the Chiefs of Staff to have it probed properly. How was it that the Navy allowed these large reinforcements to be landed, when in an affair of this kind everything depended on the Navy isolating the Island? It is necessary to clear this up on account of impending and more important operations. One does not want to worry people who are doing so well for us in many ways and are at full extension and yet it is indispensable for our success that muddles of this kind should not be repeated.[4]

Another who was upset was Wavell. Major Cooper was debriefed by GHQ MELF on his return to Egypt and overheard him say, when the details had been relayed to him in the next door office: 'I will not have men sacrificed like this.'[5]

The upshot was that a Joint Services Board of Inquiry was convened at Alexandria on 12 March. It was held at HQ 6th Infantry Division and the joint chairmen were Major-General J.F. Evetts, the divisional commander, and Rear Admiral H.T. Baillie-Grohman. During the proceedings it was revealed that, unbeknown to Cunningham, Renouf was a sick man at the time, which may at least partly explain the haphazard planning and execution. An accusing finger was also pointed at *Hereward*'s Captain for his failure to take more positive action on the night of 25/26 February. The board's view was that he should have taken steps to try and intercept and sink the Italian torpedo boats, rather than turn his back on the island in order to rejoin, which, in the event, he failed to do.

It was made very clear that at no stage had No. 50 ME Commando had the opportunity to take part in the planning, unlike in previous Commando operations, and that they had merely been presented with a *fait accompli*. While the evidence presented to the Board by the Sherwood Foresters may have given the impression that No. 50 was in a state of some disarray by the last night, this is hardly surprising, given the problems with which the ME Commandos had had to contend during the previous 48 hours.

Unfortunately, the results of the Inquiry remained 'Most Secret' for the next 30 years.[6] This was most regrettable since word soon got out that the Middle East Commandos were, at least in part, to blame for the failure. The situation was not improved by the subsequent publication of Evelyn Waugh's diaries[7] and Martin Gilbert's *Finest Hour: Winston S. Churchill 1939–41* (Heinemann, London, 1983), although in both cases correction has since been made in public.

At the time, though, there were at least some people in GHQ MELF who would have been only too happy to see the Middle East Commandos disbanded, and Adrian Simpson, with life not made any easier by his comparatively junior rank, was having to fight hard for their survival.

Typical of the attacks was the objection by 'A' Branch GHQ MELF in early January 1941 to the Fanny cap badge on the grounds that it was 'irregular'. To this Simpson replied that since the Commandos themselves were an irregular force, they had perfect justification to wear it.[8] Then, in March he wrote to Colonel Macdonald in MO9 at the War Office complaining of the problems of trying to keep the Middle East Commandos up to strength. As much as he would like to have done, he could not call on the Australians and New Zealanders, since there was an embargo on them serving outside their own divisional commands, although this does not seem to have applied to the latter with regard to the LRDG. As for British troops, taking them was 'rather like robbing Peter to pay Paul'.[9]

By this time, though, No. 50 had returned to Egypt from Crete and had been reunited with No. 52, recently returned from Eritrea. There, they and now No. 51 had been fighting a very different type of war.

CHAPTER THREE

Eritrea and Abyssinia

No. 52 Middle East Commando, which had been warned off for East
Africa on 1 December 1940, left by train from Geneifa for Port Said
on the 16th. This was all very unexpected since the Commando had
been concentrating on preparing for amphibious operations on the
North African coast and also because it was still lacking a significant
proportion of its weapons and equipment.

At Port Said, under George Young's command, they embarked on
a French ship, the *President Doumer*, bound for Port Sudan. Also on
board was 2nd Battalion Highland Light Infantry, with whom
relations were not too good, especially after it was suspected that the
HLI had stolen the Commandos' Christmas comforts of puddings,
beer and whisky. As they steamed south, so the weather became
progressively hotter, and they were relieved to land. As soon as they
disembarked at Port Sudan, the Commandos were put on a train and
learnt that they were being sent to Gedaref, the railhead for the forces
in the Gallabat-Metemma sector.

Because Kassala, which lay on the direct Port Sudan–Gedaref
line, was still in Italian hands, the train had to make a wide detour
via Khartoum. the journey therefore took three days, but since No.
52 was the only unit on the train, they were able to stop whenever
they liked to brew up and cook meals. They reached Gedaref in the
afternoon of 22 December and spent some 36 hours here sorting
themselves out and trying to make good their equipment
deficiencies. The men were paid, but this proved to be a mistake in
some respects as some of the more recalcitrant spirits got drunk and
ventured into the black brothel area. Two were knifed by the locals
and the others had to be rounded up by the officers as the Military
Police could not cope.

The officers, at least, were therefore relieved when on Christmas
Eve the Commando boarded trucks to take them to the front. They
were to come under the command of Brigadier A.G.O. Mayne's 9th
Indian Infantry Brigade, which was part of the 5th Indian Division,
in the Gallabat area. The situation at the time was that Mayne was
facing an Italian force, slightly stronger in numbers and composed
mainly of native troops. The Italians, however, were enjoying

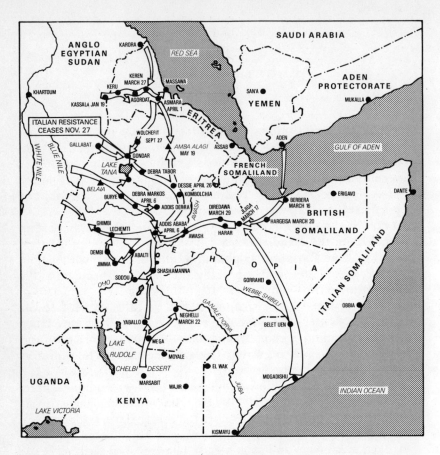

complete air superiority. Since his attacks here in November 1940 had been repulsed, General Platt had remained on the defensive, and was now awaiting the arrival of 4th Indian Division fresh from its triumph at Sidi Barrani. The plan was for 5th Indian to clear the Italians out of Kassala and then advance east to Massawa before turning south into Abyssinia. In the meantime, the Abyssinian patriots, who were being organised by Brigadier D.A. Sandford's Mission 101, were to advance from the Blue Nile south-east towards Addis Ababa, while Cunningham's forces came up from the south through Italian Somaliland.

The defence in the Gallabat-Metemma sector was, however, to be an active one and Brigadier Mayne planned to use No. 52 ME Commando as a patrolling and raiding force. On arrival, on Christmas Day, George Young found that there was little intelligence available on the enemy and that it was clear that much personal reconnaissance would be needed in order to pinpoint suitable targets for raids. He did manage to obtain a set of air photographs of the area, although, because of the air situation, it required almost every aircraft the RAF had in Sudan to escort the Anson which took them. Even so, the bushes and small trees with which the area was littered made it virtually impossible to identify enemy positions on the photographs. Indeed, this type of terrain was very different to the open deserts of Egypt on which No. 52 had trained and the commandos needed to become acclimatised to it. It was also the dry season, and the River Atbara, which marked No. 52's left flank, was reduced to little more than large pools. This was the only source of water to be had. It was also very clear that both Heath and Mayne had very little idea of the Commando role, which was hardly surprising, and there was a tendency to regard No. 52 as merely a reinforcement for their very stretched infantry battalions.

That same Christmas Day, George Young and his company commanders carried out a reconnaissance of the forward Italian positions, under the guidance of a Sudan Defence Force officer who knew the area well. Christmas lunch for all was merely bully beef, biscuits and chlorinated water. During the next few days further reconnaissances were carried out, but it was not until 4 January that the first brush with the enemy occurred. The honour fell to C Company commanded by Captain David Smiley:

> We marched in a formation we had used on our training – two scouts, an advance section, myself and runners, and then three platoons in single file. As we went down the Khor I heard bird noises coming from the tops of the very tall trees as we passed them. They seemed a bit unreal and suddenly fire opened up on us from our right and left front just as an Abyssinian fell out of a tree about ten yards away. We all fired at him but missed as he disappeared into the elephant grass. Bullets were coming at us fairly fast now, but we could see nobody. However I got a Bren to spray in all directions and I saw a native run across our front and catch a burst of the Bren. I then threw a grenade and my runners did likewise – meanwhile I had given the signal for the platoons to carry out a movement we had rehearsed several times for such an eventuality. Things were made more confused by the bush on both sides of us starting to burn fiercely. Whether this was done deliberately by the enemy or by our grenades I do not know. Suddenly through the smoke I saw an Abyssinian about ten yards away firing his rifle into the air as fast as he could reload. I took a couple of shots at him with my pistol and missed. By then one of the platoon officers came up and said he had seen the

enemy – consisting of local Abyssinian levies – in full flight and led by an Iti officer on a white horse. We decided to call it a day, as it was our first baptism of fire.

Two of the enemy had been killed for a cost of one man slightly wounded by bullets which had ricocheted off his Bren gun.

Plans were now drawn up for a long distance raid on the enemy's lines of communication between Khor Kumar and Khor Abder Razzag on the Gondar-Metemma road. To begin with, John Milman was sent out with a Sudan Defence Force officer, Sudanese guide and a camel leader to check whether the enemy was still occupying a key crossing of the road over the river. They were away for four days and reported that the crossing was unoccupied.

No sooner had Milman returned, however, than he was told that George Young was sick and that he was to take charge of the operation which was to involve two companies. He was to set up an ambush on the road some 15 miles behind the enemy lines, but was under a disadvantage of not having been involved in the planning and the fact that the country the companies had to traverse was unknown and virtually uncharted. The idea was that the companies, with each man carrying three days' dry rations, would move out to an advanced base which had been selected by William Seymour, the adjutant. They would lie up here during the second day and set up the ambush that night, returning to their own lines the following day.

They set off on 10 January. Crucial to the ability to set up the ambush by night and withdraw before first light was the time it would take to reach the Atbara from the advanced base. Because of the unfamiliarity with the terrain, John Milman decided to send out a patrol to the river, which he expected to be not much more than an hour's march away, and to delay the operation until the following night. Because of the food problem he ordered one company to hand over the balance of its rations and return to base. In the event the patrol was away for six hours and returned saying that they had been unable to find the river. John Milman thus decided that further postponement brought increased danger of compromise and aborted the operation. He sent the remaining company back to base and then carried out his own reconnaissance, locating both the river and the road. Brigadier Mayne was none too pleased that the operation had been cancelled since he had mounted a diversionary attack elsewhere. Unfortunately Milman had not been told that this was going to happen.

A few days later, though, the plan was resurrected, although slightly amended. The idea was for two companies to move to Khor Ghumsa on the night of 17/18 January and there lie up. In the afternoon of the 18th, they would then move down to the River Atbara to a pre-selected lying up place, which would have been reconnoitred by Seymour. They would remain here during the daylight hours of the 19th and then attack the Gondar road that night, recrossing the river before first light and returning to the advanced base which had been set up at Meshra Habish. Four days' worth of rations were to be carried on camels.

On the 17th, the day that the operation was to commence, came the encouraging news that the Italians had retired from Kassala towards Agordat and Barentu. Preparations went smoothly, except with the camels. That which was to accompany Seymour refused to leave the others and he was consequently forced to accompany the main body as far as the advanced base instead of making his own way independently. The march to Khor Ghumsa took much longer than expected because the camels found it difficult moving through the bush in the dark. On arrival there, Seymour left for his reconnaissance, accompanied by an Abyssinian guide, and found a suitable lying up place some 20 miles behind the front line.

On the night of the 18th/19th the main body began its march to the rendezvous with William Seymour, but the local guide they had with them lost his bearings and they spent eight hours moving in a large circle before they finally reached the Atbara five miles from where they should have been. Accordingly, George Young decided to postpone the attack for 24 hours.

On the 19th, however, Seymour's party hit trouble. Shortly after dawn, they heard sounds of firing from several directions, but whether it was parties shooting game or some form of tactical exercise with live ammunition they could not tell. It began to come closer and a sentry was posted on a nearby hill. He soon reported that a native was approaching. Seymour, Raider Hickie and the Abyssinian guide went out to bring him in, but came across an Italian officer and six native soldiers in a clearing. The guide called on them to surrender and when they did not, opened fire, killing one. The enemy returned the fire and threw grenades, severely wounding the guide in the leg. The officer and two other natives were also killed, but then the enemy brought up 30 reinforcements, too many for Seymour's little party, which was forced to beat a hurried retreat, leaving equipment and the camel behind. They carried the wounded guide as far as they could, then hid him and made their way back to the advanced base in order to get a stretcher party for him. Eventually the guide was brought back by camel next afternoon.

The main body lay up at the correct rendezvous during the daylight hours of the 20th and crossed the River Atbara at 1800 hours. Three hours later, having passed by some enemy mule lines, they reached the Gondar-Metemma road and deployed along it to set up ambushes, with George Young's HQ positioned in the middle. As C Company deployed they bumped an Italian patrol. This withdrew, but not before the company had suffered four casualties, two killed and two wounded. In view of the fact that surprise had now been lost and that there were enemy encampments nearby, George Young ordered C Company to hold its ground while B Company withdrew onto the headquarters in order to provide depth and support should C Company be attacked. This was satisfactorily carried out and an enemy machine gunner killed in the process.

C Company now came under fire once more and George Young decided that total withdrawal was the only answer. During this a number of enemy posts were bumped, one of which was overrun, with four casualties being inflicted on the enemy. Unfortunately, in the confusion one of the Commando's best NCOs, Sergeant Harrison, Scots Guards, had been wounded and left behind by mistake. Nothing more was heard of him, just a single shot some minutes after the Commandos had left the area. Eventually, having successfully disengaged, the companies were back in the base camp early on the 22nd.

In the meantime, A Company, which had not taken part in this operation, had not been idle. Positioned on a feature known as the Three Bumps, it had been ordered to carry out an attack as part of a brigade policy of offensive action in order to persuade the enemy, whom it was believed was on the point of withdrawing from the area, to do so. Meeting stiff opposition, they managed to capture a prisoner, but had one man wounded in the knee, which meant a long carry back to their base.

George Young, in his post-raid report, pointed to the impracticability of long columns of men threading their way through six to eight foot high grass and scrub in deep penetration operations and recommended that these should be carried out with a maximum strength of one company. More serious, the operation had confirmed that a significant number of men in the Commando lacked the discipline required. Indeed, he was forced to court-martial one man for 'shamefully casting away his arms in the face of the enemy', although the accused was acquitted. As a result of this he was given permission to backload a number of men, and on 30 January no less than 26 undesirables, together with a further 18 men who were unfit, were sent back to Geneifa.

During the last week of January, No. 52 continued its programme of active patrolling, but mounted only one more attack. This was carried out on the night of the 26th/27th by B Company. Their objective once more the Metemma-Gondar road, but during their approach march they came up against some strongly defended enemy positions and had a number of men wounded, all of whom they managed to get back safely. On the last day of the month it was a patrol from No. 52 which established that the enemy were finally withdrawing. Orders were given for a follow-up next day, but no contact was made with the retreating enemy, who had successfully made a clean break. The speed of the Italian withdrawal made Brigadier Mayne realise that the follow-up troops would need transport if they were to maintain contact with him. Since all that No. 52 had was camels, he decided that it would be better if the Commandos handed over this task to troops who were better equipped in this respect. Therefore on 1 February the Commandos returned to their base camp to await further orders.

They were ordered to return to Gedaref, but since no transport could be spared they had to march on their feet. Setting out early on 7 February, they arrived on the morning of the 10th, having covered a distance of 55 miles – no significant challenge by Middle East Commando standards. Here they came across No. 51 ME Commando which had recently arrived in the theatre.

Two weeks later, No. 52 entrained for Kassala. There they received new rubber-soled boots and took the opportunity to carry out some mountain warfare training in anticipation of being re-employed in the more mountainous territory of Eritrea and Abyssinia. After a few days, however, they were informed that they were to return to Egypt. Leaving Kassala on 4 March, they eventually found themselves at Tahag Camp, Cairo, from where they were sent on a week's leave.

No. 52's stay in East Africa had been brief and in many ways frustrating. True, they had seen some action and had inflicted casualties on the enemy, but it could not be said that their operations had been crowned with success. They had been sent to Sudan because of the overall shortage of troops there and not on account of their special role. There was undoubtedly a lack of understanding by senior commanders on the organisation and limitations in equipment of the Commando, and, indeed, as to its proper role. The problem of the poor calibre of some members of No. 52 also played its part, and another was that malaria became rife and some 60 men succumbed to it. Nevertheless, the Commando was now battle-experienced. It was now to undergo a major reorganisation, as will be related in the next chapter.

After the frustrations of *Compass* the idea had been mooted that No. 51 ME Commando might join No. 50 on Crete. Doubts, however, over whether *Mandibles* would be approved by the Chiefs of Staff, together with Adrian Simpson's belief that it would do no good for morale to leave the Commando idle, prompted him to offer it to Platt for service in East Africa. This was eagerly accepted and, on 24 January 1941, No. 51 sailed from Suez, bound for Port Sudan, on board the troopship *Dunera*. They arrived at Gedaref on the 30th, the day before the Italians withdrew from Metemma and Gallabat. No. 51 spent three weeks at Gedaref, which gave them a good opportunity to become acclimatised to the climate and terrain, as well as doing unit training, especially important since the Commando had been very split up until now. Much advantage was taken of the abundance of game in the area, and this provided welcome variety to the rations. On 14 February, Kid Cator travelled to Khartoum and was briefed on his role in the forthcoming operations. He was to come under the command of 4th Indian Division, which, after driving the Italians out of Kassala, had now reached Agordat and was closing up to the seemingly impenetrable fortress of Keren. It was to here that No. 51 was to be deployed.

On 21 February, the Commando was moved to Kassala and two days later was taken by lorry, under the auspices of one of the South African Cape Transport companies, to a camp ten miles west of Keren. Next day, Kid Cator reported to Major-General Beresford-Peirse, GOC 4th Indian Division.

Beresford-Peirse had been wrestling with the problem of how to get through to Keren since the beginning of the month. The road from Agordat initially passed through a narrow valley, but then traversed a wall of razor-topped ridges before dropping down into Keren itself. The Italians, realising that if Keren fell the whole of the rest of Eritrea would be quickly lost, had hastily reinforced it and had blown down some 200 yards of cliff in order to block the road as it wound through the rock barrier in front of the town. Beresford-Peirse had launched an attack to seize Brig's peak, the highest point in the range, on the night of 2/3 February. This attack was repulsed, but repeated the following night and for a few hours the feature was held. Intense mortar fire, from which there was little cover, proved too much and the attackers were driven off. Foiled here, he tried further south with a fresh brigade, but this too could make little headway.

Now, Beresford-Peirse tried a two-brigade attack on Brig's peak and its southern neighbour the Sanchil feature, but again the attackers could not hold onto the ground which they had won. Because of the hostile nature of the terrain, Beresford–Peirse had little option but to attack frontally. He now realised that for this to be successful he would need much more artillery than he had at present and therefore decided to pause while this and the necessary ammunition were collected. In the meantime, in order to close the ring as much as possible, he ordered his third brigade, which had been detached to northern Eritrea, to be brought up to Keren. This then was the situation as No. 51 ME Commando appeared on the scene.

Beresford-Peirse's orders to Cator were to institute a programme of patrolling and ambushes. These began on 25 February when Captain Rayne's troop (unlike Nos. 50 and 52, No. 51 retained the original sub-unit designation of 'troop' rather than 'company') went off to look at the ground to the south of Keren, specifically to see if tanks and wheeled transport could get through to harass the Keren–Asmara road. The other two troops moved to the hills west of Keren in the Ashisha area. There had been reports of Eritrean native cavalry operating here and the object was to ambush them by one of the water holes. Cator, realising how important these water holes were in such arid country, proposed to Beresford-Peirse that he should base the complete Commando in the Ashisha area in order to occupy them all. The divisional commander agreed to this and, having commandeered some camels and obtained the loan of some lorries, No. 51 moved to the area on the 27th.

Next day, Henry Frost had the first contact with the enemy. After occupying a group of water holes around Mansuia, Frost had pushed on towards the east and had been fired on at long range by what he estimated to be two companies' worth occupying a group of sangars. There was another contact in the same area on 28 February. As a result, Cator decided to push on up the valley towards Keren and see if he could establish himself on the Samana feature. No. 51 set off to do this in the late afternoon of 2 March. Shortly after they had started orders came through from division that one troop was to be sent back, and Kid Cator's efforts to get this postponed were to no avail. In the meantime, the firing of a red Very light indicated that Keymer's troop had bumped the enemy. Keymer:

> I expected to be ambushed, or rather to run into the enemy, so we were
> properly organised when we did just that. The two point men inevitably
> bought it, but we rapidly cleared the Italians out with grenades and
> rifle-grenades.

In addition, Keymer's troop suffered six wounded, but managed to
take some prisoners. They continued the advance during the night
and at dawn took up a defensive position on a ridge. Simultaneously
with his main advance, Keymer had sent a section under Lieutenant
James to try and get round the enemy's left flank. He returned 24
hours later, having sent back three prisoners. Once consolidated on
the ridge, Cator, who had joined Keymer after the initial contact,
stalked and shot a native soldier. Unfortunately, he did this with a
dum dum bullet – many of the officers had sawn the tips off the
ordinary service rounds in order to use them against crocodiles. As a
result, those who were carrying these modified rounds quickly got
rid of them since, of course, their use was strictly against the Geneva
Convention. Later another enemy party was spotted and subjected
to sniping fire.

The camels and mules now came up with food, water and
ammunition and it was remarkable how they and their handlers
adapted to active service, especially shell fire. At the same time
orders came from Division that the complete Commando was to
return to Divisional HQ immediately. Accordingly, they withdrew
to their forward base, where Kid Cator met Ian Lapraik, who was
acting as No. 51's liaison officer at Division. Lapraik had fresh
orders. No. 51 was to get up onto Beit Gabru, a hill just west of
Samana, and from there harass enemy observation posts which had
been creating difficulties for the infantry operating on the lower
ground. Kid Cator considered that this could be better achieved by
using the area from which he had just withdrawn. Therefore, he
immediately sent a troop back to occupy it and passed a message
back by wireless to Divisional HQ asking for permission to operate
on the north side of Beit Gabru, saying that he would like to come
back and discuss it with Beresford-Peirse. This he did that very
afternoon and returned next day. Matters were now, however,
marred by some bad news. Henry Frost's troop, which Cator had
sent back to Division on the 3rd, had been in trouble and he himself
was wounded and missing.

Frost's troop had been attached to one of the battalions of 11
Infantry Brigade. He had been ordered to scale a steep gulley

running south from Beit Gabru, harass enemy positions and deal with any observation posts that he might come across. Cator:

They set out with two days' rations and what water and ammunition they could carry. They climbed the face of the gulley during the early part of the night; the climb lasted three hours. Henry gave them a rest at the top and pointed out their objective, a saddle in between two heights, which looked like the U of the backsight of a rifle. They moved on again about 10.30 p.m. All went well for a short distance.

Suddenly, after this, they were challenged. Henry was then heard to say, 'Our presence is known, the game's up, go for them.' He and his 30 men then charged the enemy position. They soon found themselves up against wire and this in the dark. Somehow or other they got through it and swarmed the position, killing all the occupants, about 10 in number. They then reformed and found they themselves had suffered no casualties, apart from cuts and tears from the wire. They next moved on to the top of some high ground half right, and took up a position there awaiting daylight. Henry was then hoping to see what his next move would be. As dawn was breaking they were suddenly fired on by Breda and Rifle fire; then an action started which lasted nearly 50 minutes.

It soon became evident that the enemy were trying to close in on them from three sides. Mortars were brought into play and their position became very 'tricky'. Two men, Ulrich and Weinstein, were hit, Weinstein being killed outright. The fighting had by now got to close ranges. The men had thoroughly got their blood up and were fighting splendidly and showing great steadiness. The enemy's advance had now been checked by our Rifle and bren gun fire, a modest estimate of enemy dead being at least 30. Henry now realised that he was not a strong enough force to hang on, and also ammunition was running short. He therefore gave orders to [Lt] Randel and [Lt] Millard to retire while he and Sgt Heath remained back to give covering fire with their Tommy guns.

As soon as the men had reached the crest of the ridge and were under cover, he and Sgt Heath started to fall back themselves. A short distance back, they found Randel with Ulrich trying to help him out, one of his legs appearing paralysed from his wound. Henry and Randel between them started to drag the man away, Sgt Heath giving covering fire. They had gone about 5 yards when they were caught in another burst of fire. Ulrich received another bullet wound which killed him, and Henry was hit in the leg. Heath and Randel then turned to help Henry. A second or two later Henry got hit again in the body and Randel in the foot, Sgt Heath getting a graze in his left arm and the hilt of his 'fanny' saving him from being hit in the side above his hip. Henry was now down and appeared to be dying. He gave orders to Randel and Sgt Heath to leave him and get out of it as best they could. Sgt Heath again gave covering fire, until his Tommy gun jammed, at the same time giving

Randel a hand. They had about 25 yds to go to reach cover and having achieved this, they looked back to see Henry nearly surrounded by oncoming Italian black troops. He had propped himself up and was firing what was left in the magazine of his Tommy gun. This was his last effort of defiance before they saw him fall back as if dead.[1]

Frost, Ulrich and Weinstein were buried where they fell, together with 30–40 Italian troops who had also been killed in action. It was some months, however, before Henry Frost's mother established exactly what had happened – there was a rumour that he had died in an Italian hospital. Yet, when she inserted a death announcement in *The Times* the words 'attached to a Commando' were censored on the grounds that 'the existence of Commando units and their operations in any specific theatre of war may not be published until they have been officially announced.'[2] Nevertheless, Frost was posthumously Mentioned in Dispatches and Sergeant Heath was awarded the Distinguished Conduct Medal.

No. 51 continued to patrol and harass the enemy during the next few days. Cator was, however, forced to pull back to his original line for a number of reasons. Lack of men meant that he was spread very thinly and the forward water holes also proved unfit to use. He was concerned, too, about his long lines of communication. Nevertheless, there is no doubt that the commandos were causing the Italians some discomfort, as was demonstrated by their frequent bursts of artillery fire in Cator's sector. Indeed, as Beresford-Peirse told Cator on the 11th, when he went to be briefed for his part in the main attack against Keren, he had drawn two battalions' worth onto him.

The main assault on Keren was launched by 4th and 5th Indian Divisions on 15 March. While the 4th were to tackle Sanchil and Samanna once more, 5th Indian Division was to attack Fort Dologorodoc, which guarded the Agordat–Keren road on its south side. No. 51's task was to continue harassing operations north of Samanna in order to prevent reinforcements being sent against 4th Indian Division. To do this, Kid Cator decided to send one party up onto Beit Gabru to deal with enemy observation posts while the remainder of the Commando were to advance up the valley in four separate groups. They set off at 0300 hours on the 15th and all the parties experienced some action. Keymer's troop had the most involved brush.

My party reached the ridge at dawn with a higher point to the right overlooking the valley we had come up from and up which Cator was to move. I left [Lt] Lowe and the men on the ridge and went to the top with

Steve Irwin – nothing but a precipice down into the valley. One Italian soldier appeared and I got Steve to cover him as I stopped him. It took him a long time to understand that I was the enemy, but I took his rifle, bandoliers and a satchel of those rotten red banger hand grenades off him and told him he was a prisoner. Having relieved him of his encumbrance, he shot off into the darkness defiladed from Steve and me carrying all his kit!

This stirred up a hornet's nest and his friends came down at us from down on the left and also when we reformed the men from along the ridge ahead. We had a good session with grenades, hanging on to them after we had pulled the pins as 7 seconds was too long. The bangers they threw at us were ineffective. We were in an awkward position on a narrow ridge with our backs to a precipice, so we gave them a final salvo of grenades and ran straight through them. I had to come off the ridge across some open ground to another position, so I led the retreat walking, as I feared that some of the men would bolt if left on their own. It was like keeping a dog to heel, and stopping them disappearing. It got fully light after this and we had a right angle of enemy positions ahead of us in some rather exposed rocks. There was one fellow with an LMG who I had fun with. He was firing at a gap in the rocks we wanted to cross. He was too rhythmic and I slipped a man across the gap between bursts and he never hit one of us.

I had Urgar and Kramer on my LMG and the rock ahead and the ground on either side was becoming splattered, but they never shifted. I couldn't see the gun at about 450 to 500 yards as I had lost Cator's X10 field glasses. I found them and got Kramer to fire a burst at the hill. We saw the strike and I corrected him and that was the end of that Italian gun crew. They made one or two attempts during the day to attack us, but we snuffed them out before they got going.

In another incident, Sergeant Stanley climbed to the top of a small knoll on which stood two native huts. To his surprise he came across an Italian radio operator, who grabbed his rifle. In the hand-to-hand tussle which followed Stanley was wounded in the arm by a shot from the rifle, but did for his opponent by burying his Fanny in his neck, thus proving that it was no ornamental gimmick. After everyone had finally returned, in the early hours of the 16th and exhausted by almost 24 hours of continuous action and physical exertion, Cator recorded in summary in his diary:

All had done very well and we, I think, had achieved our object nobly. We had engaged and kept on 'tenterhooks' 2 Btns of the enemy all day, and had bluffed them into thinking we were a far larger force than we actually were. We had also caused them to 'loose off' a prodigious amount of ammunition to very little effect.[3]

As for the main attack, 4th Indian Division managed to get up onto Samanna, But Sanchil proved too tough a nut to crack. 5th Indian Division, on the other hand, captured Fort Dologorodoc on the 16th. In the face of fierce counter-attacks, they managed to cling onto it for the next ten days, running out of both ammunition and food and having to be resupplied by air.

Accepting that further attacks on Sanchil were unlikely to be productive, General Platt now decided to bring up fresh troops and try the direct approach, attacking down the road leading into Keren. In this way maximum advantage could be taken of 5th Indian Division's toehold at Fort Dologorodoc. In the meantime, No. 51 continued their harassing tactics, although they were now beginning to feel the strain:

> Flies and ants seem to increase daily. Most of us have got these nasty sores and the flies are continually at them, with the result that unless they are covered up they have no chance to heal. Shortage of water containers is an awful bore, as it means one can spare no water for washing and shaving. Some of the men look the most awful brigands now, with huge growths of beard.[4]

Perhaps it was their appearance at this time which caused an Indian Army officer to later describe No. 51 Commando very unfairly as 'the sweepings of Palestine, Jews and Arabs who were thieves and murderers', a comment which the most recent historian of the campaign has quoted, but made no attempt to refute.[5] Food also became short. Indeed, for some time now Jewish and Muslim culinary sensitivities could not be catered for and Philip Keymer recalls one of his men, a Jew, 'with an open tin of bacon in one hand and a fork in the other shovelling it down as fast as he could'. On 23 March there were two successes when Rayne and Lapraik cleared the Italians from two hills overlooking No. 51's valley, but on the same day the Commando HQ was spotted and subjected to accurate artillery fire. The only casualty was Kid Cator, who was hit in the left leg by a shell splinter just above the ankle and had to be evacuated. He handed over command to Gertie Miller. When Cator got back to Divisional HQ Beresford-Peirse had words of praise for No. 51, but Cator warned him that his men, having been in constant action for over a month, were now becoming exhausted and would have to be relieved soon.

As it happened, the final assault of the bastion guarding Keren took place on 25 March and was undertaken by 9 and 10 Brigades of

5th Indian Division. It was a resounding success and No. 51 were able to savour the fruits of victory by taking part in the entry to Keren. Its capture marked the unlocking of the Eritrean door. During the first week of April, 5th Indian Division went on to capture Massawa and Asmara and the country was cleared of the Italian presence.

Attention now turned to Abyssinia. The Emperor Haile Selassie, accompanied by Mission 101, had crossed the Sudanese border at the head of his Patriots and elements of the Sudan Defence Force on 20 January 1941. The ruggedness of the terrain meant that his force was totally reliant on its own feet and camels. Nevertheless, by 6 April he had reached Debra Markos, some 150 miles north-west of Addis Ababa, which he would enter in triumph on 5 May. In the south, General Alan Cunningham, brother of the C-in-C Mediterranean Fleet, had quickly overrun Italian Somaliland. Then, skirting the Harar massif, he had driven up onto the Ogaden plateau, entering Harar itself on 27 March and Addis Ababa on 6 April, two days before Massawa fell. The result of these successes was that the Italians were now reduced to holding the Galla provinces in the south-west of Abyssinia and, in the north-west, the Amhara mountains, to where the remnants of the forces which had fought in Eritrea had retreated. The Italian troops in the Amhara region were now based on three strongholds – Gondar, Dessie and Amba Alagi – and it was decided to tackle the last-named as it was considered the most decisive of the three. Platt would advance on it from the north, while Cunningham came up from the south.

Amba Alagi itself was a mountain fortress surrounded by a ring of lesser mountains. The most direct route to it from the north was from Ma Meshik and through the Toselli Pass, which was dominated by the fort of the same name. To the east there was another possible route through the Falaga Pass. Both were barred with roadblocks and any other approach would be totally cross-country, involving much climbing up hills. Another problem was that Amba Alagi was 235 miles south of Asmara, which Platt was now using as his advanced base. This meant very long lines of communication and, as before Keren, Platt recognised that he must build up his supplies before he began his move. Consequently, it would not be until the end of April that 5th Indian Division, now under command of General Mayne, who had been recently promoted from commanding 9 Infantry Brigade, was ready. In the meantime, on 26 April, Cunningham's South Africans broke into Dessie, the enemy withdrawing northwards.

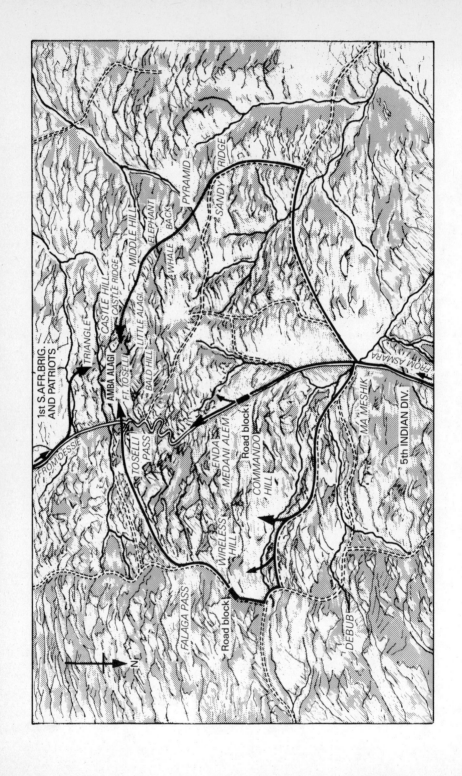

General Mayne's plan was bold. Instead of selecting either of the two roads for his main attack, he opted for a right-flanking approach, mounting feints down the obvious axes in order to draw the Italian forces away from the west. The forces detailed for that on the Falaga Pass were made up of Skinner's Horse, part of the 3/12 Frontier Force Regiment, supporting artillery and engineers, and No. 51 ME Commando. The whole was called Fletcher Force after its commander. He himself was to be promoted to command 9 Brigade during the operations, which could have caused some confusion, but luckily Fletcher Force was under this brigade's command anyway.

No. 51 had spent the month of April recuperating after their lengthy exertions in front of Keren, and were now to be given the specific task of capturing a feature which lay west of and dominated the road as it approached the Falaga Pass. This feature had no name given to it on the map and so was dubbed Commando Hill. The attack was to be launched at midnight on 30 April/1 May and the aim was to be established on the hill before first light.

Commando Hill rose to a height of some 4,000 feet and there was, as Gertie Miller later recorded, no easy ascent:

> The hill was so precipitous and rough that movement by night was difficult, while to climb slowly upwards by daylight would have been impossible in the face of enemy fire. To add to the difficulties the final upper part of the hill consisted of a cliff which certainly could only be attempted in daylight.

A patrol was sent to try and find a way up the west face, but ran into a stronger enemy patrol and had two men captured. it returned with the information that this approach was almost impossibly steep and that in any event the attackers would be subjected to fire from a hill on the left. This was why Miller was forced to make a frontal approach and by night. Finding a start line covered from enemy fire was also a problem. Indeed, there was not one to be had or a suitable approach route not in sight of the enemy. Miller therefore decided to take the most direct route and not to begin his approach march until dusk. Between 1900 hours and 2300 hours the Commando rested by a stream. They then continued the march, crossed to start line and began the long climb. Gertie Miller:

> At 0300 hours our artillery opened with a crash and for half an hour the . . . enemy positions on the forward slope of Commando Hill were subjected to heavy fire. At one moment a mass of rock was detached by

the shelling and, rolling down a thousand feet, passed through the Commando with a roar like that of an express train. By chance it passed through a gap in the ranks, but without causing any casualties. The Commando closed up again and continued their climb. At first light a position beneath the final cliff was reached and the Unit was in striking distance of success. Captain Lapraik and Major McClure succeeded in gaining a foothold on the top and were promptly engaged by the enemy.

Captain Lapraik made use of his revolver and the Commando managed to establish itself on the flat top of the mountain. The enemy had retired back and now opened fire. Captain Nemo de Sancha and his OP were captured having been completely surprised. Before he was evacuated this officer stated that we would be driven off before the next nightfall.

Defensive fire was called for and the 25 pdrs brought fire to bear about 400 yds in front of our position. This assisted us to establish ourselves and probably prevented the enemy from making an immediate counter-attack, which might have been very difficult to deal with as the scaling of the final cliff was of necessity a slow business.

Posts were established about 200 yds forward of the crest and these came under heavy fire from both small arms and the pack battery, which lost no time in avenging the captain of the Italian OP.

Major McCleod of the 3/12 Frontier Force Rifles, whose task it was to re-inforce us on our success signal, now reached the top with his magnificent squadron of Pathans. These now took over the right of our position.

Throughout the day (1st May 1941) shelling continued on our positions and the forward posts were called back to the crest at dusk. The crest was held though giving an inferior field of fire compared with the forward positions, but these proved themselves too expensive in casualties. In this operation Raider Ben Yseph was killed and nine others were wounded.

Captain Lapraik and Raider Landler were awarded respectively the MC and MM.

Throughout the day the only way in which the commandos could be supplied was by a rope anchored to one of the few stunted trees which grew on the top. That night No. 51 moved across to secure Wireless Hill, which was done without casualties. Doing this meant that wheeled transport could now be brought up to the entrance of the pass.

No. 51's next task was to further develop the feint against the Falaga Pass, again with a company of the 3/12 Frontier Force Rifles in support. This time they were to seize a position on the right of the pass itself and the operation was mounted on the night of 4/5 May.

Skinner's Horse attacked first, but were repulsed. No. 51 now tried and managed to get a foothold on the objective. Heavy fire, however, meant that they were hard-pressed to hold on to the ground they had captured, let alone move forward. After two of the troop commanders, Captains Low and Mitford-Cottam, had been wounded, Brigadier Fletcher ordered No. 51 to withdraw to Commando Hill. In spite of this setback, these actions did persuade the Italians to draw off reserves to the Falaga Pass and hence the aim had been achieved.

During this time there had been developments elsewhere. On 3 May, Bren carriers of the 3/18 Garwhal Rifles sped down the road running directly south to Amba Alagi and seized the long valley and small hills surrounding it which lay immediately north of the enemy's main defences. Early on the next day General Mayne launched his main attack. 29 Indian Infantry Brigade, in a series of quick leapfrogging actions, captured the line of hills running towards Amba Alagi from the west and was only halted by the defences on Little Alagi. To the south, Cunningham's South Africans, who had now been joined by the Abyssinian Patriots, were advancing north from Dessie.

Mayne now amended his original plan. On the night of 7/8 May he attacked Castle Ridge, the south–western shoulder of Amba Alagi, took it almost in its entirety, but was then thrown off by a quickly mounted Italian counter-attack. Simultaneously, he mounted another operation on the Falaga Pass. This was carried out by Fletcher Force, now reinforced by the 3/18 Garwhal Rifles. No. 51 successfully captured two features on the Italian right flank, Green Hill and Rump Hill, while the 3/12 Frontier Force Rifles seized Red Hill and Round Hill. The Garwhal Rifles were held in reserve and used to help consolidate the captured positions. Amba Alagi was now surrounded on three sides and the tight ring was sealed when the South Africans and Patriots successfully assaulted Triangle on 13 and 14 May.

No. 51 was now switched to the west and given orders to tackle Castle Ridge, an operation which, in Miller's words, 'would have been a tough proposition and casualties would have been heavy'. Luckily, on 16 May, the Italian commander, the Duke d'Aosta, decided that he had had enough and asked for an armistice. After two days of negotiations the 5,000-man garrison, which included four other generals besides the Duke d'Aosta, surrendered. As they marched out of the fortress, with d'Aosta the last to leave, to

pile their arms they were given a guard of honour and the men of No.
51 were privileged to be present. In summary, Gertie Miller wrote in
a letter to Kid Cator:

> We have been whisked from Brigade to brigade and called on for tasks
> which I think would have been considered difficult anywhere in the
> World. We did one attack which appeared harder than it turned out and
> were congratulated by Division on a 'splendid achievement'. In another
> night operation we got two troops on the objective and were then driven
> off, but I think we did our job as it was only a demonstration to
> concentrate more of the enemy on the opposite flank to our main attack.[6]

No. 51 Middle East Commando had without doubt made a valuable
contribution to the victories at both Keren and Amba Alagi, and
could justifiably feel pleased with themselves.

Elsewhere in Abyssinia there had also been successes. During the
first part of May, Cunningham's troops cleared the Italian forces
from the Lakes area south of Addis Ababa and were now pursuing
the remnants north-west through the Galla-Sidamo region. The only
significant enemy force left in the country was in the area north of
Lake Tana, which lay between Metemma and Amba Alagi. It was to
here that No. 51 ME Commando was to be deployed next. First,
though, they retraced their footsteps back to Adi Ugri for another
spell of rest and refitting. Then, in the second half of June came the
rains, which put a severe brake on operations. Nevertheless, on 24
June No. 51 received orders to proceed to the Wolchefit area.

The Italian resistance north of Lake Tana was centred on the
fortress of Gondar and was commanded by General Nasi, who was
determined to hold out as long as possible and had 40,000 men at his
command. Earlier, at the end of January 1941, with the Italian
withdrawal from Metemma and Gallabat, with which No. 52 had
been involved, 9 Infantry Brigade, with a scratch mobile force, had
pursued the enemy as far as Wahni, which was reached on 7
February.

Progress, however, had been slow because of the numerous mines
which the Italians had left behind en route. 9 Brigade was then
transferred to Keren, less one battalion, which was in its turn
relieved by elements of the Sudan Defence Force and Abyssinian
Patriots at the end of March. No further attempt to move forward
was made until the end of May, when an Italian battalion was
destroyed at Chelga, but this was largely negated by an Italian
counter-attack which drove the Sudanese and Patriots back to their

start line. Then came the rains. Another offensive prong had been moving north-west from Dessie and consisted of East African troops from Cunningham's force. This had reached Debra Tabor before being held up by the rains. Finally, there was the thrust from the north. The main obstacle on this route was the Wolchefit Pass, which was well defended by artillery and Blackshirt battalions.

Unfortunately, by now Platt had lost both 5th Indian Division, which had been sent to Iraq in the aftermath of the revolt there in May 1941, and the 4th. This was urgently needed in the Western Desert to help stem Rommel's first offensive. One brigade, however, was detached to Syria. There was thus little available with which to force the pass. True, at the end of May Major Ringrose and his band of patriots, who were operating west and east of Wolchefit, did manage to seize and hold Debarech, to the south of the pass for a time before being driven out. In spite of this part of Ringrose's force still remained astride the road to Gondar at Amba Giorgis.

Platt's orders to Gertie Miller were:

> You will ascertain whether the enemy has evacuated the WOLCHEFIT position. If so you will occupy a bridgehead on the South side of the summit of the pass to cover the repair of the road demolitions.
>   If the enemy is still in position, you will not attempt any frontal assault from the North but will carry out active patrolling, so far as the ground admits [sic], to locate his positions.[7]

On arrival, they were to relieve a company of the 2nd Highland Light Infantry and take the 2nd Motor Machine Gun Group of the Sudan Defence Force under command. Miller was also to make contact with Ringrose and 'arrange for such co-operation with his forces as may be possible'. No. 51 arrived in the Wolchefit area late on the 25th and the first thing that became very apparent was that the enemy was still firmly in control of the pass.

Accordingly, on 27 June, HQ British troops in Sudan and Eritrea issued a further order, this time to Lt-Colonel J.H. Needham, who was to assume command of all troops in the Wolchefit area. In addition to No. 51, the 2nd Motor Machine Gun Group and the remnants of Ringrose's Patriots, there was also a field battery. The plan was to reinforce this with a complete field regiment Royal Artillery and then to try and secure a lodgement in the pass so that the obstacles created by the Italians on the road could be cleared. The force was given the title *Necol*.[8] Later, a further reinforcement in the shape of the 3/14th Punjabis was also brought down from

Asmara, but efforts during July to force the pass failed. No. 51's main task was patrolling, but the rains and the seeming stalemate made it a monotonous time.

Nevertheless, No. 51's overall efforts in the campaign were beginning to be recognised. Kid Cator had earlier received a letter from Wavell in which he said that he had 'lately visited Eritrea and heard from more than one source of the very gallant and distinguished work which has been done by No. 51 Commando. It obviously enjoys a great reputation, and I know that the spirit which inspires it is very largely your creation'.[9] The War Office also issued some press releases on the work of the Commando, although no mention of its title was permitted. Typical of how the media presented this to the public is displayed in this piece from the Johannesburg *Sunday Times* of 20 July 1941:

SHOCK TROOPS IN EAST AFRICA

JEWS and Arabs fought side by side with Springbok soldiers in the Abyssinian campaign and shared with them the honours of many a notable victory scored against the Italians. This information has now been revealed in London in fuller reports of the concluding stages of the campaign.

The Palestinians formed a unit of shock troops, specially selected for their toughness and speed of movement. The unit was composed of 60 per cent Jews and 40 per cent Arabs, and the men serving in it came from a dozen countries in Europe and the Middle East . . .

These Palestinian shock troops were armed with 'Tommy guns and a new weapon invented during the Spanish Civil War [sic], in which knuckleduster and dagger are ingeniously combined.

The Palestinians made lightning sorties into the enemy ranks and rapidly destroyed communications. Their mobility and toughness was such that they spread terror in the Abyssinian [sic] lines.

The use of the past tense implied that the campaign was already over and that No. 51 had already left the theatre, whereas, of course, it was still in action.

Nevertheless, the days of the Middle East Commandos in Abyssinia were becoming numbered. After the failure to force the Wolchefit Pass, which eventually fell to the persistent Basil Ringrose and his patriots at the end of September, No. 51 was moved to Adowa, where it spent the last half of August and all September. In October orders were received to return to Egypt. They thus missed the final act of the campaign which took place at Gondar at the end of

November, resulting in the surrender of General Nasi and 22,000 men and the end of Mussolini's East African empire. While No. 51 had been away from Egypt dramatic changes in the organisation of the Middle East Commandos had taken place and this meant that No. 51 were to find themselves part of a very different body to that which they had known at the beginning of 1941.

CHAPTER FOUR

Crete

The return of Nos. 50 and 52 Middle East Commandos to Geneifa in March 1941 heralded a radical reshaping of the Middle East Commandos and, indeed, the overall deployment of Commandos in the theatre. The main driving force behind this was *Cordite*, the plan to capture the island of Rhodes. Z Force, the UK-based Commando brigade organised by Lord Keyes for this purpose, had finally arrived at Suez on 7 March. They had been told that they were to come under command of Major-General J.F. Evetts' 6th Division, which was responsible for the mounting of *Cordite*. Evetts himself had been the Chiefs' of Staff original choice for the post of DCO, but could not be spared from India. Such was the haste now to carry out *Cordite*, that Evetts, then commanding Quetta District in northern India, had only received a signal on 8 February ordering him to report as soon as possible to Wavell at GHQ MEF. On arrival he had been briefed on *Cordite* and told to make his new command operational as soon as possible.

One point that Wavell made to Evetts was that, for security reasons, no mention must be made of the word 'Commando' or that Z Force had any connection with the Royal Navy. Instead, Z Force was rechristened Layforce, after Bob Laycock, its commander. In order to strengthen it, Nos. 50 and 52 ME Commandos were to be made part of it. The UK-based Commandos were on a higher establishment – 500 as opposed to 370 all ranks – and both ME Commandos were now below strength. This was as a result of casualties, sickness and disciplinary action, and reinforcements were hard to come by, especially since Rommel was beginning his first offensive in Cyrenaica, 57,000 men had just been sent to Greece and the campaigns in Eritrea and Abyssinia were continuing to tie up troops. It was thus logical to amalgamate the two, and George Young, being the more experienced, was appointed to command, Peter Symons, who in any event was in his mid-forties and rather on the old side for Commando work, leaving the ME Commandos for staff post under the Engineer-in-Chief Middle East.

The Commandos in Layforce were now designated battalions and made up as follows:

A Battalion (Lt-Colonel J.B. Colvin West Yorks) – formerly No. 7 Commando formed from line regiments in Eastern Command.

B Battalion (Lt-Colonel D.R. Daly Scots Guards) – formerly No. 8 Commando formed from London District and the Household Division.

C Battalion (Lt-Colonel R.R. Pedder HLI) – formerly No. 11 Commando formed from Scottish Command and often known as the 'Scottish Commando'.

D Battalion (Lt-Colonel G.A.D. Young RE) – formerly Nos 50 and 52 ME Commandos.

The new establishment of D Battalion now reflected that of the other three battalions. It consisted of five companies each of two 50-man troops. Stephen Rose was appointed second-in-command, William Seymour adjutant, and Major John Milman, Highland Light Infantry as administrative officer. The company commanders were as follows:

A Company – Captain K.E. Hermon DLI
B Company – Captain C. Parish Royal Sussex Regt
C Company – Captain W.J. Burton York and Lancaster Regt
D Company – Captain R. Boyle The Black Watch
E Company – Captain L.N.R. Wilson Royal Sussex Regt

It must be stressed, especially in the light of subsequent events, that this organisation did not make the Layforce battalions equivalent to the ordinary infantry battalion in terms of firepower. They still lacked heavy weapons and, for that matter, the necessary transport.

D Battalion officially formed at Geneifa on 28 March 1941. Three days later, the Adjutant held a battalion drill parade, 'the first of its kind' in the Middle East Commandos, as he recorded in the War Diary. This probably represented just the experience of No. 52, since No. 50 had certainly had drill parades and had taken part in one or two ceremonial occasions while on Crete. 'The arms drill was ragged and will not be good until such time as the Cavalry members have learnt the first principles of holding the rifle and the Light Infantrymen can be persuaded not to race away with the time.'[1]

What was significant about this was that it reflected George Young's determination that his new command should be trained along more conventional infantry lines than had hitherto been the case with the Middle East Commandos. His experience in Sudan had convinced him that this form of training, rather than the original

ME Commando concept of fostering individual self-reliance at the expense of normal corporate military discipline, would make a more battleworthy unit. Besides which, Nos. 50 and 52 had had very different experiences in action, the former having concentrated on amphibious warfare and the latter on bush warfare, and it was important that the two elements were welded together.

Accordingly, Stephen Rose organised a programme of training in minor tactics at platoon and company level. This was based mainly on a series of set piece exercises which each sub-unit had to undergo. Subsequent events were to demonstrate how correct this approach was.

General Evetts was, in the meantime, grappling with *Cordite*. This was not without its problems. For a start it meant close co-operation with the Royal Navy, represented by Rear Admiral Baillie-Grohman, with whom he had sat on the Board of Inquiry into Castelorizzo, and the RAF. The latter's representative was, however, based on Crete and Evetts never met him face-to-face. He also had to run two headquarters, one alongside GHQ MEF in Cairo and the other on the Bitter Lakes, where all amphibious training for the operation was to take place.

The first positive step was taken at the end of March. No. 8 Commando had brought with them out to the Middle East a folboat section commanded by Captain R.J.A. Courtney. On arrival, he had been put in touch with Lt-Commander Nigel Clogstoun-Willmott RN, who was developing the speciality of surveying beaches from a submarine. On three successive nights they conducted a detailed reconnaissance of three beaches on Rhodes from HM Submarine *Triumph*, with Courtney paddling his Naval compatriot close inshore and Clogstoun-Willmott swimming in to examine the beaches. They brought back a wealth of information and what was especially encouraging was how unprepared for any attack the Italians seemed to be. Key personnel were also briefed on the battalion's role in *Cordite*. After an assault landing by night the ME Commandos were to capture the airfield on Rhodes. There was much studying of maps and air photographs and even greater urgency to get the Battalion trained.

On 6 April 1941, however, the Germans launched Operation *Marita*, the invasion of Yugoslavia and Greece. All available air and naval assets were needed to support the British and Commonwealth forces in Greece. While this made Rhodes a particular threat to the maritime communications between Egypt and Greece, there were now no ships or aircraft to spare for *Cordite* and it was postponed.

Within three weeks, as a result of the German Blitzkrieg, the Royal Navy was evacuating the forces sent to Greece. The Axis could now dominate the north-east Mediterranean and *Cordite* was no longer relevant and was cancelled.

Just as serious was the success of Rommel's offensive in Libya. The Western Desert Force was being driven in some disarray towards the Egyptian frontier and reinforcements were desperately needed. As a result, 6th Division was broken up and much of it, including 22 Guards Brigade and the divisional artillery, sent to the Western Desert. Layforce, singularly ill-equipped to face Rommel's tanks, was placed in GHQ reserve, but this would not be for long.

On 11 April, Laycock had received orders to be prepared to carry out amphibious raids in parties of 200 men on the Libyan coast. Next day, the force moved to Alexandria to be close to the Mediterranean Fleet, with D Battalion being quartered at Sidi Bishr on the eastern side of the city. On the 15th, Layforce received more specific orders. Raids were to be mounted against Bardia and the coast road near Bomba. Eventually, GHQ MEF decided just to mount the former and A Battalion was selected to carry it out. They embarked in the *Glengyle* and made the raid on the night of 19/20 April. As so often had been the case in the Middle East in the past, it was abortive. The majority of specific targets had been wrongly identified by Intelligence. One troop was landed by mistake on the wrong beach and taken prisoner, and an officer was mortally wounded after being shot in error by one of his men. Little was therefore achieved.

There now followed a period of intense frustration for Layforce, which in many ways mirrored that of the Middle East Commandos at the end of 1940. Raids were planned and orders given, only for them to be cancelled at the last moment. It also became very unclear as to who Layforce's true master was. Sometimes raid proposals came from GHQ MEF, at others from the Royal Navy. The Western Desert Force also had its own ideas. In this context, it is hardly surprising that A Battalion, which remained on board *Glengyle* until the beginning of May, should finally leave her with the comment inscribed on one of her troop decks: 'Never in the whole history of human endeavour have so few been buggered about by so many'[2] – a nice parody on Churchill's speech during the Battle of Britain.

D Battalion, while suffering less immediate frustration, felt rather left on one side. A Battalion was afloat, and B Battalion sent forward to Mersa Matruh. In mid-May, with Cyprus now under threat from the Axis forces in Greece, C Battalion was deployed to the island to reinforce the garrison. This left D Battalion in Alexandria, where it was now rejoined by a rather disgruntled A Battalion, but at least they had carried out an operation, albeit with little success. Nevertheless, the worsening situation in the Mediterranean and Middle East made it inevitable to all that it would not be long before the Middle East Commandos once more found themselves confronting the enemy and this gave an added spur to training. Matters were not helped, however, by the fact that D Battalion was also ordered to furnish guards for the Alexandria docks. Yet, this duty, however tedious, was not without excitement, as David Smiley recalls:

> Firstly because at this time air raids on Alex were a nightly occurrence and the docks were an obvious target. I remember three nights in particular, in each case when I was commanding the guard – a whole company at a time being used. The first was when we got the air raid warning and one ship which failed to put out the big floodlights she was using at the time. We finally shot them all out. The second time was when a German machine came over at about 3,000 feet and was caught in the searchlights. Everything fired at her – the entire Alex Ack Ack defence, the Mediterranean Fleet, my own Bren guns, and I can even remember an excited Egyptian policeman firing his rifle at her. Finally to our great excitement 3 parachutes opened out and we thought that the plane would crash at any moment but she carried on seemingly unhit out to sea and away. The next day a ship blew up on a mine (which of course were the parachutes we had seen) and Alex harbour was out of commission for a few days. I have never in my life seen so much fired at such an easy target without results.
>
> The third incident I remember during a raid was when I was visiting a guard during the raid with one of my sergeants and we passed about 30 yards from the *Warspite* which opened up with what seemed to me to be her 15 inch guns. Anyway we were both thrown about 10 yards by the blast.

In spite of these excitements, however, there was a definite morale problem within D Battalion. All members of the battalion had seen some action – either in the Dodecanese or in Sudan – but had not had the opportunity properly to prove themselves. Better trained than ever before, it became increasingly difficult to accept that they had been relegated to a quiet backwater of the war in the Middle East, the tempo of which was now quickening. Furthermore, the parent regiments of many members were now deeply embroiled in

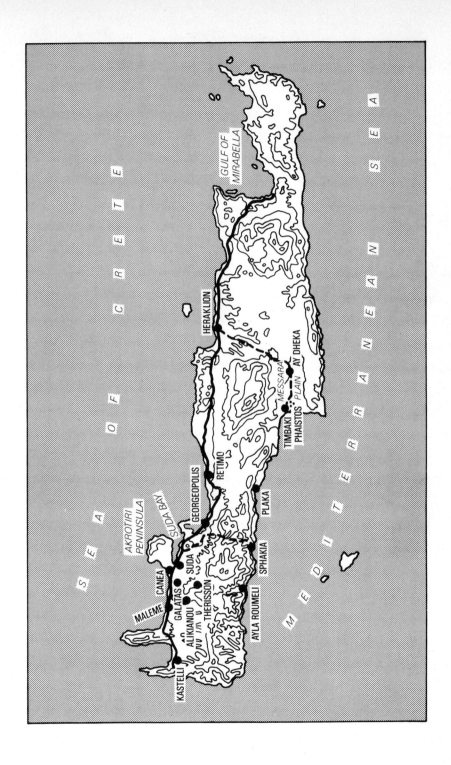

SEA OF CRETE

GULF OF
MIRABELLA

MEDITERRANEAN SEA

HERAKLION

AY DHEKA

MESSARA
TIMBAKI PLAIN
PHAISTOS

RETIMO

GEORGEOPOLIS

AKROTIRI
PENINSULA
SUDA BAY

PLAKA

SUDA

CANEA

THERISSON

SPHAKIA

MALEME
GALATAS

ALIKIANOU

AYIA ROUMELI

KASTELLI

the Western Desert. Men had joined the Middle East Commandos in the belief that they would have more chance of seeing action, but now the boot was on the other foot. There was an understandable feeling that it was the Western Desert and not Alexandria where they should be at a time when the future looked increasingly grim. There had also been a sad loss at the end of April when Stephen Rose, who had done much to introduce imaginative ideas into the training, severely damaged his left hand, losing two of his fingers, in an accident with some explosives. His place was taken by John Milman. Nevertheless, this seeming limbo was about to be rudely shattered.

On 20 May 1941 the Germans launched an airborne assault on Crete for what was to become one of the nastiest and most bitterly fought hand-to-hand battles of the war. Since March, the defence of the island had become very much the responsibility of the Royal Marines in the form of the Mobile Naval Base Defence Organisation (MNBDO) under Major-General E.C. Weston RM, although 14 Infantry Brigade, under whom No. 50 ME Commando had served during the winter 1940–41, was still in place.

After the evacuation of Greece, some 25,000 men, mainly of the 2nd Australian and 2nd New Zealand Divisions, were landed on Crete, but without much of their heavier equipment, which they had been forced to leave behind. The German success in Greece meant that the threat to Crete was much increased and Wavell decided that these men should remain on the island to help with its defence. He appointed Major-General Bernard Freyberg VC, commanding 2nd New Zealand Division, as overall commander, considering that Weston probably lacked operational experience. Conscious of his grave shortages of equipment, Freyberg constantly badgered GHQ MEF for his deficiencies to be made good. In early May, he did succeed in obtaining a number of field guns, although many of these were in a poor state of repair, a squadron of light tanks and six infantry tanks, all of which were very battle-scarred. The Germans, on the other hand, had some 500 transport aircraft, together with gliders, and 600 combat aircraft available. Of their total strength of 22,750 men (compared with an overall 30,000 British and Commonwealth troops, many of whom were base details, and 11,000 Greek defenders) they planned to land 750 by glider, 10,000 by parachute, 5,000 by transport aircraft and the balance by sea. The early seizure of aerodromes was critical to the success of their plan and, to this end, their main attack was to be mounted against Maleme and Canea, with a secondary effort, flying in later in the day, against Retimo and Heraklion.

The first attacks came in at dawn on the 20th, but by the end of that day the Germans had succeeded in gaining a firm lodgement only at Maleme. During the 21st they secured the airfield here and a counter-attack failed to wrest it back. By 24 May, although the Germans were still being held at Canea, Retimo and Heraklion, they were able to fly in reinforcements to Maleme at will and Freyberg considered that his only chance of driving them out lay in holding onto the vital port of Suda through which supplies and reinforcements, should any be forthcoming, would have to flow. Accordingly, he gave orders for his troops to fall back onto a defensive line running from the coast through Galatas, some six miles west of Suda, and thence south to the mountains.

The first indication Layforce had that its services might be needed on Crete came at about midnight on the 22nd/23rd when Laycock was told that his headquarters, together with A and D Battalions, would come under Freyberg's command for the purpose of carrying out raids on the German-held air bases in order to do something to alleviate the enemy's air dominance over the island. Both battalions were alerted and put on four hours' notice to move. Kitbags and blankets were not to be taken. The Commandos were not, however, told their destination, although, as the D Battalion War Diary noted, 'It does not need much stretch of the imagination to guess at Crete'.[3] On the afternoon of the 23rd they were transported to the docks with the intention that they should take passage in one of the Glen ships. This was cancelled at the last moment on the grounds that these were too vulnerable to air attack. D Battalion was now given the order that topees were to be worn, which suggested that they might be earmarked for somewhere other than Crete. In the meantime, there was a desperate scramble to try and find sufficient warships to take Layforce to Crete. Initially all that was available was the fast minelayer HMS *Abdiel* and she embarked 200 men of A Battalion. She sailed that night and the men were landed at Suda Bay next morning as an advance party.

D Battalion and the remainder of A Battalion were now told that they were to be landed at Selino Castelli on the south-west coast of the island. From here they were to march cross-country for 35 miles in order to take the Germans at Maleme in the flank. This seemed a tall order, especially from the resupply aspect, although such an operation was well within the Commandos' physical capabilities. To have landed on the west coast of the island would have significantly cut down the distance to be marched, but would have increased the distance by sea and the danger that the ships might be caught by enemy aircraft in daylight, since there would not be sufficient hours of darkness to complete the disembarkation and their withdrawal. This option was therefore discarded.

At first light on the 24th, D Battalion was informed that transport would arrive at 0800 hours to take them to the docks. When it did materialise there was insufficient to move the battalion in one lift. Four destroyers, HMS *Isis*, *Decoy*, *Hero* and *Nizam*, had been earmarked and they wanted to weigh anchor at 0900 hours in order to ensure that they were clear of Crete by dawn on the 25th. In the event, because of the transport difficulties, they were not able to set sail until almost 1100 hours and even then a complete troop of A Battalion had to be left behind. At about midnight, as they neared the island, a strong gale blew up and visibility worsened considerably, so much so that there was doubt whether they had arrived off the correct landing place. To make matters worse, many of the ships' boats were smashed, which meant that it would only be possible to land a small proportion of the force. Fuel, too, was running short and at dawn it was decided to abort the operation and return to Alexandria.

The commandos arrived back at Alexandria at 1915 hours on the 25th and were given fresh orders. Those on board *Isis* and *Decoy* were told to transfer to *Abdiel*, now back from delivering the advance party, and she, together with *Hero* and *Nizam*, would now take Layforce to Suda. There were, at least in D Battalion, one or two men who were not fit to march long distances, and the opportunity was taken to disembark them. They included William Seymour, who was suffering from a ruptured Achilles tendon, and his position as adjutant was taken over by Michael Borwick of the Royal Scots Greys. At 0530 hours on 26 May the ships set sail for Crete once more, this time with the missing A Battalion troop safely on board. As they left harbour they passed the destroyer HMS *Kipling* entering with Lord Louis Mountbatten and the other surviving members of the crew of her sunk sister ship *Kelly*.

In the meantime, the situation on Crete had worsened. Throughout the 25th, the Germans had attacked the Galatas position, but had been repulsed in some desperate fighting by the New Zealanders. During the next day, however, the Germans succeeded in penetrating the positions held by the Greeks on the left of the Australians and New Zealanders, and Freyberg realised that his men were reaching the limits of their endurance. He therefore recommended to Wavell that evacuation now seemed the only course open. This would have to be from the south coast of the island,

Above No. 50 ME Commando practising amphibious landings on the shore of the Great Bitter Lake.

Right Crossing the Sweet River Canal on an improvised raft.

Right En route to Crete, November 1940: members of No. 50 ME Commando on board HMS *Warspite*.

Above Captain John Pendlebury, first SOE agent on Crete, who was of such help to No. 50, but was killed on the island in May 1941.

Left No. 50 practising transshipping from HMS *Derby*. Note the ladder, the only means available for carrying this out!

Left February 1941, No. 50 on their way to Castelorizzo.

Above Landing on Castelorizzo.

Right The mail boat from Rhodes arrives in Castelorizzo harbour just after its capture. Note the two ME Commandos on the left – one has an Italian flag draped over his shoulders.

Right Overlooking Castelorizzo harbour with HMS *Ladybird* moored in it.

Left The *President Doumer*, which took No. 52 ME Commando to Port Sudan.

Left Captain David Smiley of No. 52 with a donkey captured in an ambush on the Metemma–Gondar road. It later escaped.

Below No. 52 ME Commando march through Metemma after it had been evacuated by the Italians.

Above Officers of No. 51 ME Commando at Khartoum. Kid Cator is third on the right in Service Dress hat.

Right Members of No. 51 with their camels near Keren.

Right Henry Frost's grave at Keren. The wooden cross was later replaced by a proper headstone.

Above No. 51 ME Commando officers near Keren. The figure on the left is Ian Lapraik who won an MC at Amba Alagi and then went on to have a distinguished career in the Special Boat Service.

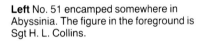

Left No. 51 encamped somewhere in Abyssinia. The figure in the foreground is Sgt H. L. Collins.

Left Crete: looking north from D Battalion Layforce's position at Babali Hani 50 years after the battle. The ground has changed little.

Above Crete: Sphakia, from where the garrison of the island was evacuated, as it is today.

Right 1st Special Service Detachment, Taungye, January 1942. Seated centre is Major John Milman and on his right (in white puttees) Jocelyn Nichols.

Right SSD 1 moves out from Kengtang, 27 April 1942, with its Chinese contract mules.

Left Arriving at the end of a day's march at a village in Yunan.

Left Fifty years on. Captain Arthur Swinburn DCM lays a wreath in the memory of the Middle East Commandos who lost their lives during the battle for Crete.

Below The Memorial to No. 51 Middle East Commando in Israel.

but he would maintain a rearguard in the Suda area in order to cover the withdrawal. There was no immediate answer from Wavell.

Layforce, ignorant of what Freyberg had proposed and of the true situation on Crete, arrived at Suda just before midnight on the 26th. Major (later Major-General) F.C.C. Graham, the brigade major:

> No sooner had the ship anchored than boats from the shore began to come alongside and, just as the Brigade Commander, myself and other officers were bidding farewell to the Captain of the minelayer [*Abdiel*], the door of the latter's cabin was flung open and a bedraggled and apparently slightly hysterical Naval officer burst in. In a voice trembling with emotion he said, 'The Army's in full retreat, everything is chaos, I've just had my best friend killed beside me, Crete is being evacuated!'
>
> Cheerful to say the least of it, something of a shock to this little party of Commando officers, armed to the teeth and loaded up like Christmas trees, who stared open-mouthed at this bearer of bad news.

The gloomy situation was reinforced when D Battalion's C Company commander, Bill Burton, bumped into Freyberg in person on the quayside. Burton was told that the battle was already lost and that Freyberg considered Layforce's mission to be pointless. Nevertheless, Layforce got on with the disembarkation, but all heavy equipment, including newly issued wirelesses, cooking equipment and Bren gun magazine boxes had to be left on board since it was clear that there was no transport available to carry them. Also *Abdiel* had been unable to come alongside the quay, which meant that everybody and everything had to be transferred via lighter to the shore. Landing the heavy equipment would have taken time and the ships were desperate to get away and be at sea before daylight because of the enemy air threat. In the event the heavy equipment quickly ended up in the sea. Only such ammunition and food that could be carried on foot was taken.

Laycock himself went to find General Weston, whom Freyberg had put in command of the forward area. Weston confirmed that an evacuation had been ordered, even though Wavell's agreement to it was not received until the afternoon of the 27th, and said that Layforce was to provide the rearguard. A liaison officer from A Battalion's advance party now turned up at the docks and passed the same message, also stating that his group, including Lt-Colonel Colvin, was holding a position to the south-east of Suda.

Accordingly, the second-in-command, Major K. Wylie RE, took the rest of A Battalion off to join them. D Battalion followed, with

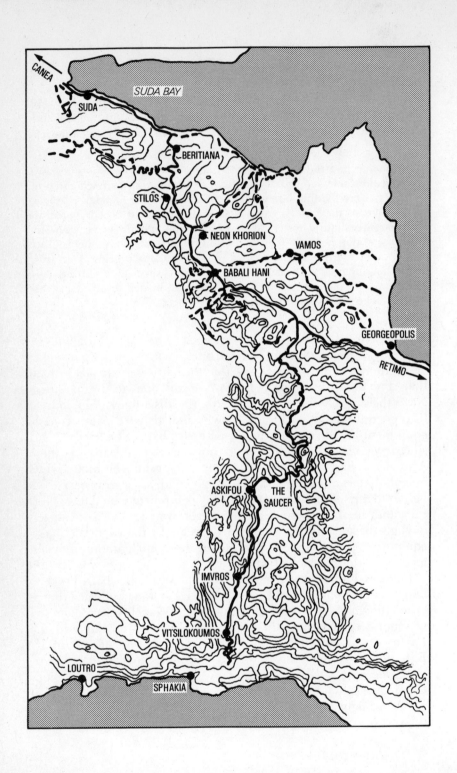

CANEA

SUDA BAY

SUDA

BERITIANA

STILOS

NEON KHORION

VAMOS

BABALI HANI

GEORGEOPOLIS

RETIMO→

ASKIFOU

THE
SAUCER

IMVROS

VITSILOKOUMOS

LOUTRO

SPHAKIA

orders to take up a position in depth on a ridge six miles from Suda and astride the road to Sphakia. George Williams, formerly Stephen Rose's bodyguard and batman and now a runner at battalion HQ, remembered that march:

> It seemed that a retreat was already in progress and thousands of men were streaming eastwards through Suda . . . We turned onto the road heading in the same direction as the disorganised retreating men, who impeded our unit. We were properly armed and formed up. We overtook four men struggling uphill with a stretcher laden with ammunition boxes. CSM Howland said, 'Come on, let's give these blokes a break.'
>
> He collared two other men and we took over. With the wooden shaft handles taking the weight on our shoulders, we carried on. We covered quite some distance and were now looking for someone to give us a break; but no help was forthcoming. Those stragglers could have made light work of that load, but they weren't having any. Before we reached our assembly place I was regretting having taken over the stretcher in the first place. the handle was really biting into my collar bone and I tried out several different things, like stuffing my hat under the handle etc., but it made no difference. It must have been the same for the others, but I heard no complaints.

It is a description that could well have come from the pen of Rifleman Harris, that veteran of Sir John Moore's retreat to Corunna over 130 years before. Indeed, there were many similarities in the two retreats. In both cases the terrain was inhospitable, the army was moving away from its supply dumps as opposed to withdrawing on them and hope for salvation lay in the Royal Navy. The only real differences were that Moore's retreat was longer and took place at the height of the Iberian winter.

At 0515 hours D Battalion arrived at its destination and three companies were deployed to cover the road. Throughout the daylight hours of that day, the 27th, D Battalion was bombed and machine-gunned from the air, but thanks to the availability of cover there were no casualties. In the afternoon George Young and Michael Borwick reported to Laycock for further orders. George Young was told to reconnoitre a position for his battalion suitable for holding the enemy. Once he had found one, he was to pull his men back to it, but leave one company to hold where the main road left the coast and turned south. This company position was tactically unsatisfactory since it was very exposed and could be easily outflanked. George Young pointed this out to Laycock, who referred the matter to Weston's headquarters, but the reply came back that it had to be done.

George Young therefore set off and found a suitable defensive position at Babali Hani, some twelve miles south of Suda Bay. That night D Battalion withdrew here, leaving B Company, which contained the Spanish Troop, with the unenviable task of holding the forward position. The battalion arrived at Babali Hani in the early hours of the 28th. George Young had previously decided to deploy all four companies in line, two on each side of the road. On arrival they deployed roughly to their company areas and at first light occupied their positions in detail, arranging inter-company junction points and tying up arcs of fire. George Young was very conscious that his left flank was rather in the air and in order to prevent himself being surprised sent out patrols from E Company, the extreme left hand sub-unit. No contact was made with the Germans.

Major R.L. McGibbon was commanding the Spanish Troop in B Company and had two subalterns under him, Russo of the 3rd Hussars and Sandbach of the Cheshires. To take up their defensive position they had to march westwards from D Battalion's original area.

> This meant marching headlong into fleeing British troops – most of them had not an officer to be seen anywhere and damn few senior NCOs. It wasn't a retreat – but a rout. I remember Lt Russo saying, 'Christ, Bob, we'll never get out of this mess,' and I silently agreed. It was hard to explain to Spaniards why British troops didn't stand and fight – or it would have been hard – had they asked the question. In any case, we took up our position . . . Young had explained the slim chances of us ever getting out, but he was very fair about it. Shortly afterwards a platoon of New Zealand Maoris came through us – commanded by a 2nd Lieutenant. All were carrying not only their own weapons but also German weapons. They asked if they could join us – for a chance to fight the Germans! They stayed and later I sent them in on a bayonet attack.

A Battalion, meanwhile, had spent the daylight hours of the 27th witnessing the withdrawal of elements of Creforce, including the 1st Welch, the only troops to escape from the Akrotiri Peninsula north of Canea. Once these had passed back through them, A Battalion received the order to withdraw themselves during the early hours as the rearguard. At dusk they were engaged by German patrols and pulled out at 0200 hours on the 28th.

After having marched a few miles, they were attacked by the Germans in the flank, which created some confusion, but passed through B Company at 0500 hours. By this time B Company had been reinforced by no less than two Maori companies and three hours later were in contact with the enemy. First they were subjected to mortar fire and then German glider troops attacked them from both the north and the south. The fighting took place at ranges of 100 yards or less, because of the scrub and broken terrain. Bob McGibbon himself was badly wounded and gave orders to Russo and Sandbach to leave him and withdraw. Later he was to have some consolation:

> After I was finally picked up by the Germans, one of their officers expressed surprise that so few commandos (although he did not know that we were commandos) had held up the German attack for so long. The German said that their losses were very high – especially the number killed.

The remnants of B Company, together with their Maori comrades, now made their way back to Babali Hani, where the remainder of D Battalion were now preparing to receive the enemy.

Michael Borwick remembered 'the constant stream of demoralised and leaderless' troops which came back through their position. Eventually the remnants of A Battalion appeared. Lt-Colonel Colvin had been taken sick and Major Wylie had been appointed by Laycock to take his place. Three troops of A Battalion were deployed to cover the left flank and took up position alongside the remnants of B Company, which had now rejoined the battalion. Also made available to provide much needed depth to the defence was the 2nd/7th Australian Infantry Battalion. General Weston had, in addition, given Layforce three of the six available Infantry Tank Mk II Matildas, which belonged to the 7th Royal Tank Regiment.

By about midday the Germans were beginning to close up to Babali Hani and the defenders came under heavy mortar fire to which, of course, the commandos were unable to reply. George Williams had been sent forward with three other men to establish an observation post forward of the main position.

> We could see quite a long way up the road along which any mechanised vehicles would have to travel. Eventually the first that came into view were Jerry motorbikes and sidecars. Our signallers passed this message with mirrors. There was a church tower some distance over the

other side of the road from which a sniper later did some deadly work. But I think someone was there already and had spotted our signals, because just after this they started peppering us with mortars. They soon got the range and were becoming quite deadly. The corporal then gave the order to get back to HQ. We started to come downhill. The mortar fire shifted and a sniper opened up. It then became a race downhill to the nearest cover, which was one of the many stone walls round there. Running downhill and leaping made for fantastic strides, some of which must have been about ten foot long, at least they felt like it.

John Milman had been visiting D Company on the right flank of the position when the action started. He immediately made his way back to Battalion HQ which was situated just east of the crossroads in the village of Babali Hani. He noted that the position had been bolstered by the appearance of a tank which was positioned behind the inn at the crossroads. Indeed, when George Young, accompanied by Stephen Rose, revisited Crete for the first time 45 years later, the villagers of Babali Hani still had vivid recollections of the tank shooting up German positions. They also remembered the first clash with the German motor-cycle combinations and described how they went hurtling off the road and into a shallow quarry. They showed Young and Rose where the crews had been temporarily buried and were told of a lady in the village who still possessed a Schmeisser sub-machine gun which had been taken by partisan relatives of hers off their bodies.

At this stage there was only desultory firing, but as Milman was sitting on a bank studying a map with George Young and Michael Borwick, he was hit in the leg by a bullet and had to spend the rest of the battle in a ditch until he could be evacuated. Arthur Swinburne was with A Company, just to the right of the main road:

> We had a grandstand view of the goings on. Watching our troops in the olive groves and the Germans in the fields until we saw field grey uniforms showing themselves coming closer. We pooped away making the contents of those uniforms crawl for cover, unfit for further service or eligible for their Roll of Honour.
>
> After a particularly hot 10 minutes of intense mortar and machine gun fire with some kind of field gun as well, the fireworks stopped as suddenly as they had started. So we dug the earth out of our ears and I went further up the hill and the officer went round his posts to see how the lads were getting on. Soon our bren gunners were engaged in a duel with German machine gunners, but this was the prelude to rush our right flank.

One of those Bren gunners was Arthur Noble:

> We never had a moment's respite. I had to keep my Bren gun in constant action. The need to estimate distance had by then gone. I dropped my sights down to zero. Boyle [his No.2] was carrying on valiantly, filling and charging magazines as they became empty, and changing barrels as they became hot. The Jerries were pressing closer and closer and just as our first box of ammo ran out they appeared to have broken through on our left.

What in fact had happened was that the initial attacks of the German 5th Mountain Division had been conducted by two battalions advancing down the axis of the road. By 1330 hours they had been repulsed and the Germans now brought up two further battalions. On D Battalion's left flank there was a ravine running roughly east-west, which provided a covered approach and it was inevitable that the Germans would take advantage of this, although they continued to maintain pressure frontally on D Battalion.

This new threat from the left began to develop from about 1500 hours. Part of the 2nd/7th Australian Infantry was moved up on the left of E Company and at the same time Laycock arrived to see what was going on. The original intention had been to hold the position until 1300 hours on the 29th, but with the main body of Creforce now clear, Laycock gave orders that D Battalion were to extricate themselves as soon as possible after dark. Battalion HQ was now being much troubled by snipers and, according to Michael Borwick, they were much attracted by Laycock's full colonel's hat with distinctive red band:

> I went down the road with Bob Laycock for him to see for himself – he was a great morale booster by himself, full of fun and made jokes all the time. One enemy fighter had a go at us, so we landed up in an undignified heap. I cannot remember who was on top.

Laycock now left, taking with him the wounded John Milman in his pick-up. In the meantime, the German thrust on the left was held off and with the coming of darkness the pressure slackened. Indeed, it was noticeable that the Germans significantly reduced the tempo of their operations once night had fallen.

The A Battalion troops left first and were clear of the position before dark. D Battalion began their withdrawal at 2100 hours. The original plan was for Layforce to take up another position during the hours of darkness to the south of Vrysos and dumps of rations and ammunition had been put here for this purpose. However, given the overall losses suffered and general exhaustion of the remaining troops, General Weston now gave orders that Layforce was to go directly to the evacuation area and take up a position guarding the right flank. 42 Field Company RE, the only engineer element on the island, had been given orders to prepare and blow a series of demolitions in the wake of the rearguard, but because of the overall confusion it was inevitable that mistakes would be made. Freddie Graham:

> There were still many wounded, all D Battalion itself and Brigade HQ eventually to be withdrawn over the mountains to the assembly area near Sphakia, so that there was as yet no question of 'blowing' the main road. Imagine my horror therefore when, on being sent back to report to General Weston, our immediate superior commander, I found a huge crater in the road which was being admired by the sapper party who had done the deed. In a fury I cross-examined the officer in charge but all he could say was that a senior officer who said that he was commander of the rearguard had ordered him to 'blow'. To this day no one knows who that senior officer was.

Hasty efforts were made to partially repair it, but it was clear that it could not be made passable to vehicles, not that Layforce really had any, but there were plans afoot to requisition local vehicles, both for the wounded and to save the commandos' legs. In the event, sufficient transport was found to take the wounded and some of the commandos as far as the crater. The withdrawal continued on through the night and during the following morning. Tim Darby, a section commander in D Battalion:

> The withdrawal thereafter was most discouraging, but we were cheered by the promise that if we could keep going in good order, we would certainly be evacuated from Sphakia. It was a question of withdrawing slowly, leapfrogging through Maoris and Australians in the mountain passes. From time to time we became involved in sporadic bursts of small arms fire. Enemy snipers were very prevalent and efficient.

With the coming of daylight there was grave concern that Layforce was very vulnerable to air attack. The road snaked through the mountains in a series of hairpin bends, with a steep ravine on one side and a cliff on the other, and thus there was hardly any cover to be had. Luckily, it was not until they arrived at their destination that the air threat really made itself felt. Another problem was shortage of food. Bob Laycock:

> I should mention that from what I saw of the regular army in Crete . . . it was badly in need of food. The rations had been reduced to one biscuit and 1/4 of a tin of bully. The commandos, however, fared better for they had been taught to live on the country and do without rations and I never saw any of them faint from hunger, though some of the regular soldiers did so. For example after the battle I have mentioned [Babali Hani] my servant gave me two roast fowls for dinner, with rice etc. The scrounging of food was done by the Spanish Foreign Legionaries, that formed part of the 52nd Commando [sic]. They refused to fight our sort of battle but had no objection to foraging and turned out to be remarkably good cooks. They scrounged oil, rice and red pepper, goats, pigs and chickens.[4]

The implication that the Spaniards were not interested in fighting is not very fair, bearing in mind the creditable performance they had put up, but they were clearly better trained at living off the land than their British comrades. This is not to say that all of Layforce enjoyed the same high culinary standards as their commander. Arthur Swinburn describes a meal that he had during the withdrawal:

> 27 men into one tin of sausages (one tin contains 13) so each man had half a sausage leaving the 27th man, poor blighter, with the tin, some fat and the smell of what was once there!
>
> As the senior in each case had to distribute the ration, imagine how unlucky I was! But I did better on potatoes. 9 into a tin of potatoes left one over for me. Army biscuits were distributed 1½ biscuits per man. This was the first food we had had for a very long time.

The truth of the matter was that in the first place the original garrison had become over swollen as a result of the evacuation from Greece and there had not been sufficient time before the invasion of Crete to bring in sufficient stocks of food. Furthermore, as has been previously pointed out, unlike most withdrawals which normally take an army back through its own supply depots, in Crete all these were in the northern part of the island and mainly centred on the port of Suda and virtually nothing had been previously dumped in the south.

At 1500 hours on 29 May D Battalion arrived at the village of Askipho, its assembly area prior to taking up its duties as right flank perimeter guard. Now came a short opportunity to rest while reconnaissances of the new position were carried out. This was, however, much disturbed by machine gunning by marauding German aircraft. Bob Laycock, meanwhile, had reported to General Freyberg, whose headquarters were now located in a cave at the foot of the Sphakion Ravine. Freyberg told him that the order of evacuation was to be fighting troops, followed by stragglers, and that Layforce was to be the last of the regular troops. That night they took up position at the mouth of the Sphakion Ravine. George Young deployed three companies, A, C and E and kept the remainder in the ravine itself.

As for the overall situation on Crete at this time, Heraklion and Retimo had continued to hold out. Indeed, the Australians at Retimo had made some very successful counter-attacks, recapturing some ground, but suffering heavy casualties. Unfortunately, they had no communications with Freyberg's headquarters, now in the Sphakia area, and it was not possible to arrange for them to be evacuated. The force at Heraklion was, however, successfully taken off by the cruisers *Orion* and *Ajax* on the night of the 29th/30th, apart from the wounded who had to be left behind.

As for the main evacuation itself, Sphakia was and still is a tiny fishing village with just one mole and a small crescent beach and much resembles Mullion Cove in south-west Cornwall. There was thus a limit to the number of men that could be taken off. Freyberg's original plan was for 1,000 men to be evacuated on the night of the 28th/29th, 6,000 the following night, 3,000 the next night and a further 3,000 on the night of 31 May/1 June. Layforce was to be taken off on the last night.

The Royal Navy's main concern was the safety of its ships. It had already suffered casualties during the evacuation from Greece and it was now to lose even more heavily. Of the squadron built round *Orion* and *Ajax*, which took off the Heraklion garrison, two destroyers were sunk, including the Middle East Commandos' old friend *Hereward*, and three ships badly damaged as a result of repeated air attacks. No less than 800 of the original 4,000 survivors of the garrison became casualties. On the first night of the evacuation from Sphakia, the Royal Navy, because of the adverse air situation, would only embark men between midnight and 0300 hours. As a result only 700 men were taken off, although some urgently needed supplies were landed. On the night of 29/30 May the target of 6,000 men was reached, but HMAS *Perth* was damaged, and the following night only 1,500 men could be evacuated in four destroyers and two of these were damaged. Freyberg now called for an all out effort for the final night.

In the early afternoon of the 31st, Layforce received orders to hand over their task on the right flank of the evacuation area to the Maoris and to come in closer to the village and beach of Sphakia. Before he himself took off in a flying boat for Egypt, Freyberg also told Laycock that his force was not expected to defend the perimeter to the last man, but that there would be no withdrawal without orders from HQ Creforce. He stated, though, that Layforce would now be embarked after the fighting units, but before the stragglers. Later that evening Freddie Graham reported to General Weston.

General Weston asked me if I had paper, pencil and carbon paper – quite remarkably I was able to reply in the affirmative thanks to that old friend the Army Book 153 which was still in my haversack. On my reply General Weston said, 'Sit down on that suitcase and take this letter at my dictation, make three copies.' He then proceeded to dictate the capitulation of Crete!

The order itself was addressed to Lt-Colonel Colvin, who was present in Weston's headquarters at the time. As to the exact wording of the order, there is some confusion in that three separate versions (all given at Appendix IV) exist. They all, however, are essentially the same. Freddie Graham again:

General Weston took two of the copies I had made, handed one to the officer concerned [Lt-Colonel Colvin], put the other in his pocket and with the words: 'Well gentlemen, there are one million drachmae in that suitcase, there's a bottle of gin in the corner, goodbye and good luck.' He walked out of the cave and down the hill into the darkness. Later he was flown out by flying boat which had been sent to fetch him – he was forced to go under order from GHQ Cairo.

I was left staring at the miserable piece of paper which, only too forcibly, confirmed our worst fears. There was to be no further evacuation after that night and already the ships were in Sphakia bay and were filling themselves to bursting with weary troops; but there were many thousands more. Rousing myself I went out of the cave and shouted for the Bde SM [Brigade Sergeant Major] telling him to gather together crew for a Motor Landing Craft which I had seen on the bank and which I had every intention of trying to lay my hands on with a view to sailing it down the east coast. Just after he had gone to do this the

Brigadier [sic – Laycock], whom I had not seen all day came panting up the hill.

Laycock first of all explained that he had obtained orders for himself, Graham and Evelyn Waugh, the Layforce Intelligence Officer, to return to Egypt. The grounds for this were that he still had two battalions of his command elsewhere in the Middle East. According to Freddie Graham, Laycock had seen Weston earlier and one of the latter's staff officers had pointed out this fact. This would explain why the surrender order was addressed to Colvin and not to Laycock. It is also probable that, given the fact that Colvin was obviously not well enough to handle such a delicate matter, Laycock took matters into his own hands, HQ Creforce having now left, and had the order amended so that it was addressed to the 'Senior officer left on the island'. For the time being he held onto it himself and concentrated on the business of trying to get as many of his men off the island as possible.

Freddie Graham sent a runner to George Young with a message telling him to withdraw his men for embarkation and D Battalion began to move down to the quay. There was no contact with the enemy at this time and so it was a relatively easy matter to disengage. The closer to the quay they got, however, the greater the problem with stragglers and it proved more and more difficult to make any headway against the milling crowds of leaderless and confused men. Laycock and his staff did their best to try and delay the sailing of the last remaining ships, but at 0245 hours the Senior Naval Officer decided that he could not remain any longer without severely jeopardising the ships' safety and weighed anchor. Laycock, Graham and Waugh embarked in HMS *Kimberley* and a total of 23 officers and 186 other ranks of Layforce managed to get off. Laycock's last action was to get the surrender order passed to George Young, who received it at 0300 hours.

The accusation could well be made that Laycock had deserted his men, but his actions, whether they were of his own volition or on General Weston's orders, were justified. For a start, as has already been pointed out, half of Layforce still remained in being and he and his headquarters were required both to possibly coordinate their actions in future operations and also to replace and rebuild that part which had been left on Crete. Bob Laycock himself later said: 'I am not sure in cases like that that the Commanding Officer should behave in the same way as the Captain of a ship and be the last to leave.'[5] George Young, who, after all, was left 'holding the baby', remains strongly of the same opinion. While battalion commanders are duty bound to go into captivity with their men in such situations, formation commanders, because they have no direct contact with the troops under their command, are under no such onus.*

When the news percolated through to the men of D Battalion that they were not going to be evacuated it took time to sink in. Arthur Swinburn:

> The lads took the disappointment surprisingly well, but wondered what would happen next? Fritz was not too far away. They stood around in the dark talking and even laughing and joking about the prospect of becoming prisoners of war. They had no inkling of what inevitably was to happen to them.

Michael Borwick offered to go with his commanding officer to negotiate the surrender, but George Young 'kindly' refused.

> He told me to go and tell the soldiers. I did so. My voice broke. I was near to tears. Corporal Coleman (Hampshires) put his hand on my arm and said, 'It's all right, Sir, we know it's not your fault'.

Borwick was not the only one to be moved to near tears. Tim Darby described one young officer as weeping 'not for himself but for his every man'. George Young had given orders for suitable materials to be found to be made into white flags and for all weapons to be smashed. He also gave permission for any who wanted to do so to try their luck in breaking through the German cordon and taking to the mountains, or to see if they could find suitable craft to get themselves back to Egypt. Some, as will be recounted in the next chapter, took advantage of this, but the majority were perhaps too numbed by bitterness and grief. The bitterness was not directed at the Royal Navy, whom it was appreciated had done everything they could to

---

* There is an interesting exception to this rule. Lt-Colonel Ian Stewart MC, Commanding Officer of the 2nd Argylls in Malaya, was ordered to report to Wavell, now Commander-in-Chief American British Dutch Australian (ABDA) Command, prior to the fall of Singapore on 15 February 1942, to brief him on the best methods of jungle fighting. Stewart had been very realistic in training his men in jungle warfare and they performed extremely well. This was helped by the fact that many of them had fought in two campaigns on the North-West Frontier of India in the mid-1930s. His men therefore went into Japanese captivity without him. He himself was made a Companion of the Distinguished Service Order for his performance in Malaya.

get the defenders of Crete off, but at those who had decided on surrender. Laycock pointed to bad beach organisation. He went on to query whether evacuation was the right answer, bearing in mind that the air cover was not available and that the 15,000 men who were taken off were 'already considerably demoralised after the evacuation of Greece'.

George Young, while accepting that the evacuation could not be prolonged after the night of 31 May/1 June, profoundly disagreed with the other reasons for surrendering, namely shortage of food, ammunition and troops capable of continuing resistance. Certainly D Battalion and the Australians and New Zealanders who made up the rearguard would have carried on fighting just as fiercely and would have welcomed another crack at the enemy. The Middle East Commandos' sterling performance at Babali Hani had shown that, in spite of being totally outgunned, they were more than a match for the enemy. At a cost of three killed and 15 wounded, they had, on the evidence of those who later had to dig the graves under German supervision, killed at least 80 and possibly as many as 200 of the enemy. The number of wounded was probably many more. The actions of the rearguard had enabled the evacuation to take place, but at the cost of the majority of its members being left behind on the island.

Sadly, as Freyberg had recognised when he spoke to Bill Burton on the quayside at Suda, the issue had already been decided by the time Layforce eventually landed on Crete. Thus all they could do was to help salvage what could be saved. While historical 'ifs' are usually a fruitless exercise, it is worth examining what Layforce might have achieved if the heavy seas had not prevented a landing at Selino Castelli (otherwise known as Paleochora) on the night of 23/24 May. Their task would have been to attack the Germans in the Maleme area and these would have entailed a march of some 35 miles over a mountain barrier and then along the side of a deep ravine before climbing up another range and descending to Maleme itself. While the original German plan involved Selino Castelli being occupied by the 24th, the heavy fighting between Maleme and Suda Bay had prevented this. Therefore the landing would have been unopposed.

It is unlikely, however, given the air situation that Layforce's presence would have remained undetected for long and they would have been subjected to air attack, without the necessary heavy weapons to be able to reply, during the daylight hours. This would have slowed them down considerably. Furthermore, the terrain provided ample opportunities for ambush. Even if they had eventually reached Maleme, they would have lacked the strength and weaponry to recapture the airfield and it is unlikely that they would have achieved any more than merely prolonging the fighting in the north of the island by a couple of days.

True, during the first two days of Operation *Mercury*, as the Germans called the Crete operation, they had had serious doubts over their progress and Student even considered aborting the operation. Once they had seized Maleme and could fly in reinforcements the die was cast, especially in view of the overwhelming air supremacy which they had enjoyed from the outset. Indeed, it is possible that Layforce would have found themselves in an even more parlous position. They would have been isolated from the main forces, their supplies would have quickly run out and the Royal Navy would in all probability have had no ships to spare to evacuate them.

That D Battalion's achievement was recognised by Laycock was reflected in the Layforce War Diary. While it stated that the equipment and special training of Layforce made them unsuited to the type of operation which they were called upon to carry out on Crete, there was praise for George Young's foresight in giving D Battalion conventional infantry training[7]. Elsewhere, Laycock spoke of the way in which George Young had 'greatly distinguished himself' at Babali Hani. This was later recognised in the award of the DSO to him and other decorations to his officers and men. D Battalion had done all that had been asked of it, but this was of little consolation to most of its members as they now began what was to be four years of captivity.

CHAPTER FIVE

The Latter Days

For those members of D Battalion who had been left behind in Egypt because of sickness or physical unfitness, the battle for Crete was an anxious time. While the fighting was going on they had no idea of what was happening to Layforce, but once the evacuation had begun and the ships, many bruised and battered from incessant air attacks, began to arrive at Alexandria harbour it became increasingly clear that all was not well. Stephen Rose, now temporarily out of hospital with both eardrums perforated and his arm in plaster, remembered looking in vain for officers and men of D Battalion and finding none. Not until Bob Laycock himself arrived on 1 June was the situation clarified, and then it was with the sad news that almost all had been left behind.

At this time, given the few members who had managed to get back from Crete – two officers and 25 other ranks, including 15 Spaniards – D Battalion had a total strength of seven officers and approximately 60 other ranks, most unfit for active duty. The remnants of A Battalion were just as slender and hence the two were amalgamated under the command of Stephen Rose on 2 June. The new unit was given the rather unglamorous title of 'Layforce Details'. Two days later, however, Stephen Rose was forced to return to hospital and his place was taken by Captain Jocelyn Nicholls RA, whose troop of A Battalion had been one of those present at Babali Hani and who, together with some of his men, had managed to get back.

There were, of course, the other two battalions of Layforce which were still intact. They had not been idle. B Battalion was still based at Mersa Matruh, but was now sending detachments on a regular basis to Tobruk, which had been under siege by Rommel since mid-April. C Battalion on Cyprus had been alerted for an operation and had sailed back to Palestine, to where they had originally been deployed, at the end of May. The reason for this was the invasion of Vichy French Syria, which was mounted in the early hours of 8 June. C Battalion's task was to carry out an amphibious landing on the coast and seize a vital bridge over the Litani River. This they just failed to do, but nevertheless acquitted themselves well, especially a certain Major Geoffrey Keyes, Royal Scots Greys, but suffered 123 casualties including Lt-Colonel Pedder killed.

Those who remained behind on Crete fell into two groups, the evaders and the prisoners of war. The prisoners, once they had been gathered together, were made to retrace their steps along the road running north from Sphakia. George Williams remembers that journey well:

That was quite some march. The men were hungry, though we were to become much more hungry before we got our next meal. It was hot and we got thirsty and water needed some finding. You'd come to a well only to find that so many people had been before you, that the well was dry. What was enough for the normal routine of the island couldn't cope with the sudden burden of thousands of walking sponges. Now it meant you had to get a move on and try and get nearer to the head of the column to stand a chance of getting a drink. One night we laid down in ditches alongside the road to get a couple of hours' sleep. Troops and vehicles were still passing backwards and forwards when one of our fellows stretched his legs out and they were crushed by a vehicle's caterpillar tracks. Another unforgettable thing was coming round a bend and seeing a burnt out truck standing on the road, five or six soldiers, obviously the crew, were sitting quite naturally leaning back against a tree and one was sitting forward peering through a fork in the trunk. All were dead but unmarked. They must have dived for cover and got caught by the bomb blast.

Occasionally they heard sounds of shooting up in the hills and the former members of No. 50 ME Commando were convinced that this must be the work of John Pendlebury. Sadly, this was not so. He had, in the autumn of 1940, set about organising a resistance movement among the Cretan hillmen and had even managed to obtain a number of small arms and some ammunition from No. 50. He was well aware of the imminence of the German invasion and had, just prior to it, gone across to Kasos to try and find out the exact date from Greek contacts whom he had living among the Italians there. On his return to Heraklion, the German invasion had already started. He landed in the harbour and made his way to his quarters, where he stayed just long enough to get his kit, rifle and ammunition together, and then set off to join his guerrilla patriots in the cave-ridden area of Mount Ida.

En route, he and a Greek reservist soldier had a successful brush with German reinforcements being dropped by parachute, but a little further on clashed with another body and he was seriously wounded. He was taken to the house of a Greek doctor and treated there, but then it appears that the Germans, realising who he was, came back for him. He was, so witnesses said, shot in cold blood in the yard outside. Even so, rumours persisted throughout the period of occupation that he was still alive and his name remained an inspiration to Cretan resistance. So concerned were the Germans that they twice exhumed his body to check on his glass eye. After the war his body was disinterred and he now lies buried in the British War Cemetery at Suda Bay.

Eventually the prisoner of war column arrived at Maleme, where the prisoners were employed to clear up the airfield. From here they moved to Suda and were taken by ship to Corinth and then to a POW camp at Salonika. Most of the wounded were diverted to a hospital in Athens, where, according to Bob McGibbon, 'conditions were pretty grim, no beds, little medical care and food very scarce. Indeed we seemed to rely on food the Germans had captured from the British. I remember getting lemon jelly for breakfast on one occasion!'

McGibbon also noticed that the Germans showed an undue interest in the Fanny and once brought one round the hospital, asking if anyone had been equipped with it. In fact, the Middle East Commandos had been warned not to be caught with their Fannies after capture and, as George Williams says: '. . . at the bottom of a well near Sphakia there are enough knuckleduster knives to start a souvenir shop.' This was, of course, long before Hitler's infamous Commando order of October 1942 by which all commandos who fell into German hands were to be killed immediately, but there was a very real suspicion that the Germans might not take kindly to any known commandos whom they captured.

The Spaniards had an additional problem in this respect and feared for what might happen to them if the Germans discovered that they had fought on the 'wrong side' in the Spanish Civil War. Luckily for them, D Battalion's medical officer, Captain A.L. Cochrane RAMC, who had also fought on the Republican side in the war, came up with an ingenious suggestion. Henceforth, the Spaniards pretended to be Gibraltarians, a ruse which the Germans seem to have swallowed.

Conditions at the camp at Salonika, to which the wounded were also sent, once they were fit enough, were also very bad. Food was scarce and disease rampant. Tim Darby:

The bugs were ferocious and, for the first time, we became acquainted with lice. A flame applied to the seams of our trousers extinguished some of them with a slight plop but their attacks caused ulcers and deep sores, particularly on those who became weaker with attacks of dysentery. There were a number of people who just seemed to give up, and deaths, although not numerous, were regular.

Nevertheless, he and others were bent on escape. In his own case, he, together with some Australians and New Zealanders evolved a plan which made use of the sewers running under the camp. On the night in question, the Germans discovered what was afoot and flooded the sewers, shooting a number of would-be escapers. Luckily for Darby, this was before his turn to enter the sewers came. To counter these escape attempts, the Germans made the prisoners spend the night crowded in the centre of the prison area. This suited Corporal J.D. Coutts, formerly of No. 52 ME Commando, and his friends, who also planned to use the sewers. From the citation for the Military Medal which he was later awarded:

> They had noticed the opening of a sewer in the centre of the camp and seen that it was wide enough for a man to crawl through. A Greek workman promised to take the lid off another opening several hundred yards from the camp as soon as it was dark. They blocked the pipe from the latrines to the sewer and turned on all the taps there and in the washhouse and left them on all the afternoon.
>
> The fact that all the prisoners of war had been pushed by the sentries to the centre of the camp provided an excuse for their presence by the sewer opening, and Coutts and several others climbed down and crawled along. It took them two hours. Corporal Coutts is broadly built and twice stuck in particularly narrow spots. The artificial washing down they had given it made a considerable difference to the conditions, but even so two of them passed out as soon as they reached the opening and fresh air. They waited until they came round and then split up into parties of two and three.

Receiving food and shelter from local Greeks wherever they went, Coutts and his two companions eventually reached safety.

After some months, all those at Salonika were taken by train to Germany, where they were to endure further privations in camps here and in Poland. George Young himself landed up in Colditz, where from October 1941 until February 1944 he was Chairman and head of the Escape Committee, as well as the Escape Intelligence

Officer, and as such helped to mastermind many of the spectacular escape attempts made from the castle.

A large number of men did try to evade capture and some were successful. The *Glengyle*, which had been involved in the evacuation from Sphakia, had left three of her motor landing craft behind and these all managed to reach the Egyptian coast. One of them, *MLC 69*, laid up until dark on the day of the surrender and then sailed away under heavy machine gun fire. Striking a rock just off Godovous Island in the early hours, those on board spent the next day scrounging food and water before finally setting out for Egypt. They ran out of both after a couple of days and became very weak. Some extracts from their log are as follows:

4th June – Spirits very low first thing in the morning at not sighting any ships but brighten up during the day. Getting very hungry but can last 3 or 4 days yet.

5th June – A few planes flew overhead too high to be signalled to or to be recognised.

6th June – No food at all but we dipped our fingers in a tin of margarine and then in some loose cocoa we had. Nerves very bad but still keeping up our spirits.

7th June – Nothing at all to eat; we are very hungry and weak. A few planes flew over but could not be recognised.

8th June – No food or water; everybody so weak that we can't stand up, but just lie around. Spirits are getting very low. At about 1200 hours we hold a church service and sing the National Anthem.

   At 1300 hours we sight LAND [sic] and our spirits rise again to there [sic] fullest extent. A plane flew over. We recognised it as a British plane who [sic] dips in salute. 4 men decide to build a raft so as to get to shore quickly so as to get help but it was a washout.[1]

Nevertheless, at 0200 hours on 9 June they did eventually strike land at Sidi Barrani, luckily in friendly territory, nine days after setting out from Crete. In the party were fifteen members of A battalion and seven of D, all of whom reported to Layforce Details on the following day. Evelyn Waugh based an episode in his fictionalised autobiographical trilogy *Sword of Honour* on this successful escape. Others were not so lucky. Major Wylie, who had taken over command of A Battalion after Colvin had fallen sick and was, like George Young, later awarded the DSO, took a small party of men and climbed up into the hills to the west of Sphakia and then down to Port Lutro, hoping to find a boat. There were some fishing boats about, but that afternoon German bombers flew over and sank them all. Wylie and his party now found themselves cut off by German troops and were forced to surrender.

Some other adventurous spirits made for the mountains. Here through SOE agents operating with the Cretan resistance fighters, wireless contact was established with Egypt and submarines came across to take the survivors back to safety. Three who escaped this way were Richard Boyle, who had commanded D Company, one of his subalterns, Dick Carr, and the acting company sergeant major, Sergeant R.J. Crooks. Boyle was killed later in the war, during the Rhine crossings in March 1945, but Crooks was later awarded the Distinguished Conduct Medal for his part in helping others down this particular escape route. In particular, it was his organisation on the beach in getting parties of men out to the submarines in difficult weather conditions.

Arthur Swinburn, who knew the island well, having been based here with No. 50 in the autumn of 1940, had the advantage of being able to speak some Greek. He had also made some good friends among the local population in the north of the island. After some days of working his way along the coast in a fruitless attempt to find a boat, he decided to journey to Heraklion. A bad attack of dysentery delayed him, but he was well looked after by a Cretan who had spent some time in America. He was then diverted by news brought to him by his host to the effect that there was a group of soldiers led by a major, who had set up camp in the mountains nearby. Meeting a fellow member of D Battalion, one of the cooks, they joined this group for a few days, but then the cook said that he wanted to visit his fiancée in Heraklion and Swinburn agreed to accompany him.

In a village just outside the town Swinburn recognised a police sergeant whom he had known earlier. The latter greeted him like a long lost friend. Unfortunately, the policeman was now thrown into a predicament by one of the few pro-Axis Cretans, who declared that he would inform the Germans that there were two British soldiers in the village. The police sergeant therefore had to pretend to arrest Swinburn and his comrade. Eventually, after many adventures, including further near escapes from capture, Swinburn was taken off the island by a Royal Navy caique at the end of October 1941 and returned to Egypt. He has never forgotten the help given him by the Cretans. 'They are simply the grandest, kindest, most big-hearted people I have met or ever wish to meet.'

To return to the overall situation in the Middle East in mid-June 1941, while the Syrian campaign was successful, even though the French put up greater resistance than expected, the problem of Rommel knocking at the gates of Egypt remained. Churchill was applying pressure on Wavell to launch a counter-offensive in the Western Desert. In May, a rather half-hearted effort to recapture the Halfaya Pass, Operation *Brevity*, had failed. A month later, Wavell mounted a more ambitious operation, *Battleaxe*, which was designed to relieve Tobruk, but this found the attacking troops back on their start line after three days' fighting. The truth was, given the losses in Greece and on Crete, and the demands of Iraq, Syria and Abyssinia, that the Western Desert Force, soon to be retitled the Eighth Army, was simply not strong enough to launch a major offensive against the Axis troops in Libya at this time. This problem over manpower was now to affect Layforce and the Middle East Commandos.

In mid-June Wavell gave orders that Layforce was to be disbanded. The grounds for this were that the Royal Navy, because of its recent high losses, was no longer prepared to make ships available for amphibious operations, the Commandos' prime role, and also that there was no prospect of the manpower being made available to make good the heavy losses of the two Layforce battalions on Crete. Formal disbandment took place on 15 July 1941, but it was by no means total. C Battalion was to continue in being in its garrison role on Cyprus, which it had now resumed, and part of B Battalion had a temporary stay of execution since it was still involved in raiding the Axis lines at Tobruk. Courtney's folboat section, which was now under Cunningham's command, was also saved. Likewise, No. 51 ME Commando remained unaffected since it was still heavily embroiled in Abyssinia. The Middle East Commando Depot at Geneifa was also maintained, both to supervise the disbandment of Layforce and to continue to supply drafts to No. 51.

The last commander of Layforce Details was John Milman, who had been fortunate enough to be evacuated from Crete with his wounded leg, and in mid-July he took the remnants of A and D Battalions to Geneifa. The majority were posted back to their parent regiments, but another option was to volunteer for guerrilla operations in the Far East.

In all five officers (John Milman and William Seymour from D Battalion and Jocelyn Nicholls, Denis Ford and Sammy Samuels from A) and some 90 other ranks were accepted for this. Part of the spur was a financial inducement, which was later repudiated, but more it enabled a sizeable body of the Middle East Commandos to continue to serve together. The story of what happened to them appears in the next chapter, but in the meantime they were designated C Troop of Layforce and left Egypt in mid-July.

Laycock himself was ordered back to England, disgruntled at the break-up of his command, but he would soon return to the Middle East.

On 10 July 1941, Colonel Dudley Clarke, who, in June 1940, as Military Assistant to the CIGS had been largely responsible for the formulation of the original Commando concept and had now been posted to the Middle East to take charge of deception, wrote to a friend of his in MO9 at the War Office: 'I am afraid that the history of Special Service Troops in the Middle East has been a sad one.'[1] He was not the only one to hold this view. The Prime Minister addressed a minute to the First Sea Lord and General Ismay for the Chiefs of Staff Committee:

> We sent these three ships [Glen] all round the Cape with much heart-burning in the hopes of *Mandibles* and other island attacks.
> The Commandos have been frittered away, and are now disbanded. The late regime in the Middle East showed no aptitude for Combined Operations. There was no DCO, but only a lukewarm and uninfluential committee.[2]

Apart from his disappointment at the way in which the Commandos had been handled, although he was clearly thinking of the UK raised element of Layforce rather than the Middle East Commandos, this was also an attack on Wavell, whom he had replaced by Auchinleck on 22 June. He followed this outburst with a further minute dated 23 July 1941 to Ismay and the Chiefs of Staff:

> I wish the Commandos in the Middle East to be reconstituted as soon as possible.
> Instead of being governed by a committee of officers without much authority, General [sic] Laycock should be appointed DCO with his forces placed directly under Admiral Cunningham, who is to be charged with all Combined Operations involving sea transport and not exceeding one brigade.
> The Middle East Command have indeed maltreated and thrown away this valuable force.[3]

By this time Laycock himself had arrived back in England and he admitted to agitating for the disbandment of the Commandos in the Middle East to be halted,[4] and this certainly reached Churchill's ears since Laycock stayed the night of 19/20 July at the Prime Minister's country residence, Chequers.[5]

At the end of July, Auchinleck himself returned to England for a brief visit and dined with Churchill on the evening of the 30th. Two weeks later, the Prime Minister sent yet another minute to Ismay:

> I settled with General Auchinleck . . . that the Commandos should be reconstituted, as far as possible, by volunteers, by restoring to them any of their former members who may wish to return from the units to which they had been dispersed. The DCO and the Commandos will be under the direct command of General Auchinleck.
>
> This cancels the former arrangement which I proposed of their being under the Naval Commander-in-Chief.[6]

By this time Auchinleck and Laycock were back in the Middle East. Laycock, however, rather than being promoted in order to carry out the role of the DCO, had lost his acting rank of full colonel and was now a lieutenant-colonel once more, which did not bode well for the future of the Commandos in the Middle East. As it was, it would be some months before the shape that reconstitution should take became definite.

In the meantime, C Battalion was formally disbanded on 1 September, but the rump of it, commanded by Geoffrey Keyes and made up of those who still believed that they had a future in Special Forces, remained in being. The same happened to the detachment of B Battalion which had been at Tobruk and which returned to Geneifa on 20 August.

The first attempt to grapple with the problem of how to keep the Commandos in the Middle East in being came in the form of a minute dated 11 September from the Deputy Director of Operations GHQ MEF to Auchinleck. Reviewing the history of the Commandos in the Middle East, it pointed to the many amphibious operations which had been planned but had been cancelled for naval reasons. It concluded that too many Commandos had been raised in the first place with not enough work being given them to do. This had resulted in loss of morale and applications by many to return to their units.

For the future, the Commandos could be employed in amphibious operations, either large or small scale. In the former, which would be carried out by armoured and infantry formations, the Commandos could be used in the airborne role or landed from the sea to attack the enemy in his flanks. Small amphibious raids could be launched against the North African coast and in the Aegean and, possibly, eventually from Turkey, should she finally enter the war on the British side. Because of the nature of the various coastlines and the lack of suitable ships, such operations would have to be limited to 40–50 men. Hence a Commando of 250 men would be sufficient.[7]

In the meantime, thanks to the initiative of a junior officer of No. 8 Commando and B Battalion, a new Special Forces unit had been formed, L Detachment Special Air Service Brigade. During a spell in hospital after a parachuting accident, David Stirling had pondered on what had gone wrong with Commando operations in the Middle East. He concluded that the concept of employing relatively large bodies of men was unproductive. Instead, he evolved a new plan for a raiding force built on four-man teams, with each member being highly trained, who could infiltrate the enemy lines and attack landing grounds, supply lines and headquarters. Eventually he managed to obtain Auchinleck's ear and was given permission to raise a force of 65 men and allotted the use of five Bombay transport aircraft. The idea was that his force should be dropped by parachute behind the Axis lines two days ahead of the launching of Auchinleck's planned major offensive against Rommel, *Crusader*, which was to take place in November.

Now, at a conference called by the Deputy Director of Staff Duties GHQ MEF on 11 October, it was proposed that the reconstituted Middle East Commando should be formed from L Detachment, the remnants of Layforce, No. 51 ME Commando and Courtney's folboat section, which was now based at Malta. The Commando was to have six troops organised as follows:

No. 1 – Depot Troop
No. 2 – L Detachment SAS Brigade
No. 3 – Layforce remnants
Nos. 4 & 5 – Palestinians (ex No. 51 ME Commando)
No. 6 – Folboat Section (Now called Special Boat Section)

It was to be divorced from G(R) Branch and the Long Range Desert Group and Laycock was appointed to command it.

There were, however, snags with this organisation. For a start, it could not be properly implemented until No. 51 had returned from East Africa and enjoyed a well earned leave. There were also serious differences between G(R) and G(Operations) branches at GHQ

MEF over who should have control over the Special Boat Section. Since G(R) Branch remained the controlling office of all 'cloak and dagger' operations in the Middle East and this was what Courtney's sub-unit had been largely employed on, the Branch felt that it must retain some measure of control over it. Laycock, too, was dissatisfied, considering that the force was too small and its component parts too disparate to be effective. In reply to his objections, the Chief of Staff GHQ MEF wrote on 30 October:

> The real difficulty of SS [Special Service] troops is that we simply have not got the men, and we are now thousands of men short of requirements in ordinary infantry battalions in the Middle East! I have told the CinC [Auchinleck] that I really cannot recommend calling for volunteers for an SS unit in view of this shortage. But this does NOT [sic] mean that when we get reinforcements we shall not be able to expand the SS organisation.

He also stated that Auchinleck wanted to discuss the matter personally with Laycock.[8] Impending operations were, however, to prevent Laycock from doing this for some weeks and the final decision on the future of the Commandos in the Middle East was held in abeyance.

Apart from Stirling's role in *Crusader*, which was to raid Axis landing grounds in the Gazala–Tmimi area in order to destroy aircraft on the ground, the rump of Layforce was given another task in connection with the offensive. This was to attack enemy headquarters and communications installations in the Cirene area of the Cyrenaican 'bulge'. The remnants of C Battalion, now calling themselves No. 11 (Scottish) Commando once more, were earmarked for this. The story of the raid, Operation *Flipper*, has been told many times. Suffice to say that Laycock and Keyes were in command, but that only a proportion of the force could be landed from submarines because of rough seas. They attacked a house, which was believed to contain Rommel's headquarters, on the night of 17/18 November and inflicted casualties, although Rommel himself was not there and never had been since it was merely a logistic headquarters. Keyes was mortally wounded during the attack and was subsequently awarded a posthumous Victoria Cross.

The survivors of the raid made their way back to the coast, but found rough seas once more, which prevented the submarines from taking them off. They now tried to get back to their own lines on foot, but almost all were killed or captured by hostile Arabs. Only

Laycock and a sergeant eventually made it back and then not until Christmas Day.

Four days later, the future of the Middle East Commandos was finally resolved. Laycock himself now severed his connection with them, being ordered back to England on that very same day to take command of the Special Service Brigade, in which were grouped all the UK-based Commandos. The reconstituted Middle East Commando was instead to be commanded by Lt-Colonel J.M. Graham DSO MC, Royal Scots Greys. It was to take over the old ME Commando Depot at Geneifa and was to be made up of the few surviving remnants of Layforce and No. 51 ME Commando, now ready for action once more, together with the Special Boat Section, which was now split between Malta and Alexandria. Roger Courtney, however, like Laycock, was ordered back to England, to raise No. 2 SBS, and his place was taken by Major Mike Kealy who had commanded the Layforce B Battalion detachment at Tobruk.

Stirling's L Detachment, whose first operation on the eve of *Crusader* had, like Laycock's, not been a crowning success, was now removed from the ME Commando organisation and placed directly under Auchinleck's command. It would, however, go on to win increasing laurels.

The Long Range Desert Group was also removed from G(R) Branch and given the same status. The Branch, however, had the consolation that the ME Commando was placed under it, but with the Ministry of Economic Warfare (MEW) Mission in Cairo, which was responsible for SOE operations in the Mediterranean countries and Middle East, having overall control. The reason for this was that an entirely new type of role had been devised for the Middle East Commando.

The German invasion of Russia in June 1941 and its spectacular initial successes created the prospect of a double envelopment of the Middle East, from Rommel in the west and a thrust southwards down through the Caucasus and/or Persia and into Iraq and Syria. *Crusader* had been successful in driving Rommel out of Cyrenaica, but the threat from the Caucasus remained. This had led to the joint British–Soviet occupation of Persia in August 1941 and the formation of the British Ninth and Tenth Armies in Syria and Iraq/Persia respectively.

Turkey, however, remained neutral and was even more determined to do so after the occupation of her neighbour. If the Germans did thrust down from the Caucasus it was very likely that they would certainly overrun Turkey, whose forces were ill-equipped to combat a Blitzkrieg attack, and might well get into the other countries as well. In the event of this happening, it was crucial that they be kept as far east of the Suez Canal as possible and one way to do this would be to encourage the indigenous peoples to wage guerrilla warfare in the enemy's rear. To do this they would need positive British support and the skills devevcloped by the Middle East Commandos would be ideal for this form of activity, which was the cornerstone of the SOE charter. Hence the reason for giving the MEW Mission overall control, although it was accepted that if the operations were taking place in an Army area, as opposed to well behind the front line, they would be directed by the military headquarters concerned.

Initially, the Middle East Commando was to consist of four operational squadrons, but it was possible that this establishment could be increased by one or more Indian, Dominion or Allied squadrons. A squadron was made up of a squadron HQ and three troops each of two officers and 26 men. A troop itself normally operated in three seven-man sections and, in all, a squadron had a strength of eight officers and 82 other ranks. Three squadrons – A, B, and C – were wholly British, but the fourth, D Squadron, was made up of the Palestinians of No. 51, together with the surviving Spaniards. There was also a Holding Depot Squadron (E), with an establishment of one hundred all ranks, of whom almost 50 per cent were officers. Finally, there was the Special Boat Section, with an establishment of 12 officers and 44 other ranks, and an attached Royal Signals section. In all, the total strength of the Middle East Commando was some 650 men.

The reorganisation began immediately, at the beginning of January 1942, and Gertie Miller, formerly commanding officer of No. 51, was appointed second-in-command. There was a plan to train a proportion as parachutists and C Squadron was moved to Kabrit for this purpose in mid-January. Otherwise, apart from training, the Middle East Commando's main function in its early days was to provide 'anti-pilfering' patrols in the docks area at Suez, something which the ME Commando Depot had been doing since the previous November. In mid-February, A Squadron was sent to Syria to prepare for a possible German invasion of Turkey. Should Syria itself be overrun, A Squadron was to operate as 'stay behind' parties in order to provide support for indigenous guerrillas operating against the enemy's lines of communication. The ME Commando also began to interest itself in another field at the end of

February, when two officers and twelve other ranks were sent on attachment to the Long Range Desert Group.

In March 1942 there were a number of changes. First of all, the Commando was moved from Geneifa to Burg el Bab. There was also a reorganisation among the Palestinians. Some 50 were sent back to the AMPC and an Arab Troop was formed under Ian Lapraik from some of the remainder. The rest, German-speaking Jews, were formed into a new and very unusual unit which was given the cover name 'Special Interrogation Group'. In the words of Colonel Terence Airey, who was now running G(R) Branch:

> It is intended that this sub-unit should be used for infiltration behind the German lines in the Western Desert under Eighth Army. The strength of the Special Group would be approximately that of a platoon. The personnel, a proportion of which have already been selected, are fluent German linguists. They are mainly Palestinians of German origin. Many of them have had war experience with 51 Commando. They will frequently be dressed in German uniform and will operate under command of a British officer [Captain Buck] who has already proved himself to be an expert in the German language.[9]

Buck himself had been serving with the Punjabis, but had been captured by the Germans. Escaping from his captors, he managed to acquire an Afrika Korps uniform and was surprised by how easy it was to pass through the Axis lines and it was this that gave him the idea of forming this clandestine unit. Aryeh Shay, a veteran of No. 51, was an early volunteer and describes his training:

> 'The Special Identification Group' [sic] was situated somewhere at the far end of an isolated end of a group of desert encampments. These men, who had turned overnight into soldiers as an annihilated company of the Afrika Korps, with all their uniforms, ammunition and documents, had received no promises. On their volunteering, Captain Buck had warned them that their lives would depend on their ability to wear their disguise faultlessly, to learn to perfection the slang prevalent among the soldiers of the Afrika Korps, and to drill in accordance with all the German methods. 'If your true identity is found out', said Buck, 'there is no hope for you.'
>
> In this way Aryeh Shay turned into a member of this secret extraordinary unit. Its contacts with other British units were nil. He was trained with great accuracy by two real Germans, named Esser [Essner] and Brueckner, who had volunteered to work with the British. He was

awakened at daybreak by the roar of '*Kompagnie, aufstehen!*' [Company, get up!]; he trained at all hours of the day and night in the use of all kinds of German weapons; he was put to tests by sudden questions in connection with his German identity, and was taken to the mess-room goose-stepping, which was partly ridiculous and partly terrifying.

Essner and Brueckner were, in fact, former members of the French Foreign Legion, but although they professed themselves to be passionately anti-Nazi and carried out their training role well, they were not trusted by members of the SIG and, as we shall see, this was borne out by later events.

A further change in March came at the end of the month when B Squadron was split up. Two troops were sent, on the orders of Eighth Army, to be attached to one of the armoured divisions, while the remainder, together with Lapraik's Arab Troop, joined C Squadron, now at Jiarabub. By now Auchinleck was bent on forming additional Commando units. The first of these was the Libyan Arab Force Commando, which was formed in March 1942 by Major Vladimir Peniakoff and later became better known as Popski's Private Army. This consisted of a small group of Senussi tribesmen from the Libyan Arab Force, with British NCOs, and its role was to operate behind the Axis lines in the Jebel Akhdar, carrying out guerrilla activities and gathering intelligence. There were also plans afoot to raise an Afridi irregular battalion and an Indian Commando Squadron.

Increasingly, however, the Middle East Commando found itself locked into the Eighth Army, as opposed to SOE, and this caused Terence Airey much concern. True, the Western Desert was now very much the focus of attention. Although *Crusader* had forced Rommel out of Cyrenaica, it was not for long. Towards the end of January 1942 he bounced back, catching the Eighth Army, many of whose units had withdrawn to the Delta to refit, by surprise. It was driven out of the Jebel Akhdar and back onto the newly created Gazala Line. For both sides Malta was now seen as the key. Auchinleck was under pressure from Churchill to recapture the airfields in western Cyrenaica as soon as possible so that pressure from the air on the island could be relieved, while the Axis were drawing up plans for a further offensive in North Africa, designed as a curtain-raiser for an operation to capture Malta. There was, however, a lull of almost four months before either side made a positive move in Cyrenaica. As part of the British preparations, though, A Squadron of the Middle East Commando was brought back from Syria and later sent to reinforce the LRDG.

This, and the fact that it was now proposed to move the ME Commando base further west to Mersa Matruh, thus even deeper into the Eighth Army's area of interest, caused Airey to address a minute to the SOE controller in Cairo in mid-April. He emphasised that the Middle East Commando had been raised to carry out fifth column work, which he defined as 'all forms of subversive and sabotage work, in and out of uniform, in territories occupied by the enemy or, in certain circumstances, which required specialist and not ordinary troops'. He pointed out that the 'Commando' title was retained only because 'it provided a suitable cover name and, secondly, since it was understood to be the Prime Minister's wish that Commandos should exist in the Middle East'. The ME Commando was, he stressed, under the direction of SOE Middle East and Balkans, although SOE would keep the C-in-C MEF informed of all activities and allow him use of sub-units, if available. He was concerned that both the transfer of A Squadron from Syria and the proposed move to Mersa Matruh would mean that the 'northern front' and the Balkans would now be ignored. He was also clearly upset that G(R) Branch had only been informed of the plans to raise the Afridi battalion and Indian squadron at a very late stage and that GHQ MEF had liaised over this direct with the ME Commando without going through him. Furthermore, since it appeared that these units would have a more 'conventional' Commando role, he wondered whether it made sense for them to come under his branch and hence the SOE umbrella.[10]

While Airey was not able to stop the move to Mersa Matruh, which took place on 26 April, he was able to convince GHQ MEF that a further rationalisation of Special Forces in the Middle East was required. The result was that in mid-May the decision was taken to drop the title 'Middle East Commando' in favour of 1st Special Service Regiment, thus emphasising the fact that the unit carried out 'special', as opposed to 'raiding', operations for SOE. It was also confirmed that GHQ MEF had no direct control over it. As for the raiding forces, these now consisted of L Detachment SAS, which had now grown to three squadrons – two British and one Free French – and various Indian, Afridi and Libyan Commandos, all of which, apart from the last-named, existed only on paper. It was now proposed that all these should be controlled by a Commando headquarters. There was also a third category of Special Forces,

'Assaulting Forces', which were to comprise airborne units, again none as yet formed. The other Special Force units in the theatre were the 11th Royal Marine Battalion, which came under the C-in-C Mediterranean Fleet, although controlled to a large extent by the Director Combined Operations in the Middle East, and the Special Boat Section, also now under the C-in-C Mediterranean Fleet. Finally, there was the Long Range Desert Group, which had been under GHQ MEF for some months past, but with operational control of it being exercised by Eighth Army. Before, however, the Special Forces organisation could be developed any further, Rommel attacked the Gazala Line on 27 May and the Eighth Army was soon involved in heavy and critical fighting which would see it driven, by the end of June, back into Egypt to the El Alamein line, the last defendable position before the Delta.

A Squadron 1st SS Regiment and the Special Interrogation Group both found themselves committed to operations during June, but the remainder of the SS Regiment was held in reserve. A Squadron under Major W.A. Knowles RE had been sent to Siwa, the LRDG's forward base, and from here they set out on 4 June with orders to carry out offensive action against enemy transport, dumps and personnel on the Barce–Slonta and Barce–Beda Littoria roads in the Jebel Akhdar. In all, the squadron had eighteen trucks organised into two patrols of five trucks each, a heavy section, which carried the necessary supplies of food and water, and a small headquarter section. They succeeded in establishing a forward base in the area and identified two likely targets, an Italian fort and a police post.

Disaster now struck. On 10 June, one patrol lost four out of five of its trucks to air attack, although there were no casualties to personnel. Undeterred, Knowles was still determined to attack the two targets, but once again they were spotted from the air. Five trucks were destroyed, including that of Knowles, who had accompanied the patrol, and the sixth wrecked its steering gear on a boulder and had to be abandoned, after being set on fire. Again, there were no casualties, but the party was now faced with a long walk back to their forward base.

Luckily, the next day, G1 Patrol of the LRDG, which was also operating in the area, had been alerted by the plumes of smoke from the burning trucks, and had sent out a vehicle to investigate. This picked up three members, including the LRDG navigator who had accompanied A Squadron. These three had been on their way to the advanced base, having left Knowles and the rest lying up in a wadi. G1 Patrol's forward base happened to be very close to that of A

Squadron and the three were able to reach it quickly on foot. Borrowing two of the LRDG's trucks, they then tried to find the rest of the party in order to bring them back, but this proved more difficult than expected and it was not until the early hours of the 16th, after firing Very lights and lighting a fire, that contact was made. A Squadron then returned to Siwa in its remaining trucks, arriving there on 18 June. A few days later both they and the LRDG were forced to evacuate Siwa in view of the Eighth Army's withdrawal back into Egypt in the face of a seemingly unstoppable Rommel. From this time onwards, however, A Squadron was gradually absorbed by the LRDG.

The Special Interrogation Group had a slightly different task. A vital convoy was en route to Malta and due there during the second week in June. It was imperative that the enemy air threat be reduced as much as possible in order to ensure the convoy's safe arrival. One way of doing this was sabotage of airfields, the SAS speciality. Accordingly, Stirling drew up a plan for attacks on six airfields – one at Benghazi, three in the Derna area, one at Barce and the last at Heraklion on Crete. The Free French squadron was selected to carry out the operation and the attacks were to go in on the night of 13/14 June. Since the Axis presence in the Derna area was particularly heavy, the services of the SIG were enlisted for the first time. The idea was that the SIG should transport each of the French patrols onto its respective airfield in captured Afrika Korps trucks.

With the obvious exception of Heraklion, the operation was mounted, as with A Squadron, from Siwa. The SAS and SIG set out on 6 June with, for the first four days, an LRDG escort. Then, and only then, did the SIG now change into their German uniforms. Herbert Buck was dressed as a private soldier and Brueckner and Essner as NCOs. Aryeh Shay, who was driving one of the trucks, was masquerading as 'Corporal Schubert':

In the afternoon they saw a roadblock. A skinny Italian soldier wearily waved his hand and asked for the pass word. Captain Buck was non-plussed for a moment. The British intelligence people had supplied them with all the information except for the password, which had been changed that week [they in fact had that for May, but not for June]. He looked at Brueckner, and the German took the hint. 'You are holding us up!' roared Brueckner in German. 'I'll report you to your superiors! Get out of the way* Don't you see that German soldiers are coming back from the desert?' In less than a minute the whole convoy was past the roadblock. In the evening the convoy met another roadblock. A fat

German corporal came running to Buck's car and told him, breathing heavily, that it would be preferable for them to park in the transit camp; driving at night had become very dangerous, panted the German. 'You doubtless know that the British Commandos reach out even here. . .'

Buck thanked him and drove the car towards the transit camp; the men got down, filled the trucks with fuel, chatted with the German soldiers, bought some provisions at the local canteen, and Corporal Schubert even stood in line waiting for supper. Shortly afterwards, the cars moved quietly on their way, unobserved in the busy and noisy camp.

During all this time the Frenchmen had remained hidden in the back of the trucks.

Next day, the 13th, the party moved up to the vicinity of the airfields and carried out a rough reconnaissance of two of them. Two of the sabotage parties were to be taken to their airfields in the same truck, driven by Brueckner. Passing through Derna itself, Brueckner stopped the truck on the pretext that it was overheating and went to a nearby German guardroom. The next that the French knew was that the truck had been surrounded and they were ordered to get out. They were not, however, prepared to give up without a fight and came out with guns blazing. In the melee that followed, their commander, Lieutenant Jordan, managed to escape and one of the SIG men blew the truck and himself up with a grenade. As for Brueckner, he was flown to Berlin and decorated with the Deutsche Kreuze in gold.

Jordan got back to the rendezvous, where he met Buck and the other patrol, which had not succeeded in penetrating its airfield and after waiting seven days in vain for further survivors, they contacted the LRDG and returned to Siwa. The SAS had more success at Barce and Benghazi, destroying a number of planes without loss. The Crete party also had success, but were betrayed while waiting to be taken off the island and only Earl Jellicoe, who had accompanied the party as a new recruit to the SAS, and a Greek guide escaped.

Throughout the first half of June there had been desperate fighting between Rommel and the Eighth Army, but, by the 16th, Rommel had the upper hand. Two days later, he invaded Tobruk, which surrendered on the 21st. In the meantime, the Eighth Army withdrew to the Egyptian frontier. For a few days there was a plan to stand at Mersa Matruh, but Auchinleck now stepped in, relieved Ritchie, then commanding Eighth Army, and took over the battle himself, resolving to defend at El Alamein, the last defensible position before the Delta. Should Rommel succeed in breaking through here the plan was to continue the fight from Palestine, but Cairo and the Delta would not be given up without a fight and troops were scraped together for this purpose.

Among those units called upon to defend Cairo was the Middle East Commando, which had now been renamed 1st Special Service Regiment so that there should be no confusion over its role. These units were placed under the command of Major-General Pete Rees, then commanding British Troops Egypt, but later to distinguish himself as a divisional commander in Burma, in what was aptly called Reesforce. 1 SS Regiment was sent to help defend Alexandria and eventually John Graham found himself commanding what was called Z Brigade. A fellow brigade commander was none other than Kid Cator, who since recovering from his wound received at the head of No. 51 at Keren had been commanding the SOE school at Haifa.

During July there was continuous fighting on the El Alamein line. Auchinleck succeeded in fighting Rommel to a standstill, but his efforts to take to the offensive himself failed. Then, in August, Churchill decided that fresh blood was required and Auchinleck was relieved by Alexander, with Montgomery taking over the Eighth Army. It was not, however, until September, after Montgomery had repulsed Rommel's final effort to break through, at Alam Halfa, that Reesforce was finally disbanded. By this time part of 1 SS Regiment was involved in another operation.

The problems of control and coordination of Special Forces in the Middle East remained, however. In early August 1942 John Graham wrote to the Director of Military Operations (DMO) complaining that the SAS, SBS and 1 SS Regiment were not being used to their full capacity and that far too much time was being spent by individual representatives pestering formation headquarters for operational tasks. He suggested that all three units should be brought under the umbrella of his headquarters, with the three operational SS Regiment squadrons – A Squadron had by now been absorbed by the LRDG – being trained as parachute saboteurs[11]. The matter was taken up by General Dick McCreery, Alexander's Chief of Staff, who agreed with the proposal to combine all three units, but not in the form suggested by Graham. In a minute to Alexander he noted that 1 SS Regiment had not been employed operationally for some time, which was not altogether so, at least in A Squadron's case, and that its previous experiences, and here he rather unfairly hearkened back to Castelorizzo, which had hardly been the fault of No. 50 ME Commando, and the Litani River, in which C Battalion Layforce had only just failed to achieve their objective, had been 'not a conspicious success'. He therefore proposed that all three units should be combined under David Stirling's command, pointing out that the SAS had been very successful and that its morale was high[12].

What both he and Graham, for that matter, had forgotten was that 1 SS Regiment was under the control of SOE and, unlike the SAS, which came under GHQ MEF, and the SBS, now controlled by the Director of Combined Operations Middle East, Admiral Maund, was not in the gift of GHQ MEF to order in this way. In any event, 1 SS Regiment was now being called upon to participate in another operation.

Almost within days of the arrival of Alexander and Montgomery in the Middle East a fresh set of Special Forces operational plans had been drawn up. These were designed to interfere with the Axis lines of communication and prevent them from building up their supplies, thus making it easier for the Eighth Army once it was ready once more to take to the offensive. By the end of August there were four firm plans. *Nicety* involved the Sudan Defence Force striking from the Kufra oasis, which had now become the LRDG's forward operational base, to seize Jalo as a forward SAS base. Another envisaged the LRDG raiding Barce airfield, while the SAS were to attack shipping in Benghazi harbour (*Bigamy*). The last of the plans, *Agreement*, was the most complicated and ambitious and was designed to destroy the coastal defence guns, harbour installations and fuel storage tanks at Tobruk. It was to involve, among other units, both 1 SS Regiment and the SIG.

Agreement called for three separate forces, which were given the names of A, B, and C. Force A was made up of 11th Royal Marines Battalion, which was to be landed from destroyers north of the harbour. Force A, consisting of a company of Argyll and Sutherland Highlanders, a machine gun platoon from the Northumberland Fusiliers, together with sappers, AA elements, signallers and RAMC personnel, was to be landed from MTBs in the southern part of the bay which makes up the harbour of Tobruk. Force B, on the other hand, was to come in from the landward side of the town. This was to be commanded by Lt-Colonel Jock Haselden, a G(R) Branch officer and noted Arab linguist who had already distinguished himself in his forays behind the enemy lines disguised as a Bedouin. Indeed, he had been involved in *Flipper*, the abortive raid by the rump of No. 11 Commando on Rommel's supposed headquarters, being responsible for reconnaissance and guiding Laycock, Keyes and their men to their objectives. Haselden's force was made up of five officers and 32 other ranks from D Squadron 1 SS Regiment under Major Colin Campbell, who had Arthur Swinburn, having joined the Middle East Commando after his escape from Crete, as his sergeant major, a detachment of the SBS under Lieutenant Ronny Langton, a veteran of B Battalion Layforce's operations at Tobruk during the summer of 1941, and the SIG. The LRDG were to be responsible for getting the force to Tobruk and they would set out from Kufra. The role of Buck's men would be that of Germans escorting freshly captured prisoners (the rest of the force) into Tobruk.

The operation was to take place on the night of 13/14 September 1942, but Force B assembled at Kufra some time before this. Those taking part in *Agreement* did have their doubts on it. For a start, it was considered that the plan was unnecessarily elaborate, especially in terms of trying to coordinate three separate forces with no overall commander. More serious was the security aspect. It seemed that far too many people in Cairo knew about it and it was the subject of idle gossip.

Nevertheless, on 6 September Haselden's force left Kufra, escorted by David Lloyd Owen's Y1 Patrol of the LRDG. After four days' travel they arrived at a spot which put them within a day's journey of Tobruk and lay up. The vehicles were camouflaged with Afrika Korps markings and rehearsals carried out. Unfortunately, Campbell now fell a victim to dysentery, but insisted on carrying on. On the morning of the 13th they set off once more, with the raiders hidden in the back of three SIG trucks. They succeeded in getting through the Axis lines, which were manned by Italians in this sector, and then set about their tasks of securing beachheads for Forces A and C. This was accompanied by a heavy RAF air raid on the town in order to distract the garrison.

Forces A and C were due to land at 0200 hours and this was to be dependent on a signal from Langton. The task of securing the beachheads took slightly longer than anticipated and Langton was a little late with his signal. It was now that things began to go wrong. The MTBs did not see the signal and had navigation problems in negotiating the bay. Only two MTBs were able to land their troops, by which time the enemy was thoroughly aware of what was happening and was sweeping the bay with searchlights. The remainder of Force C' landings were therefore aborted. By this time, the Royal Marines in HMS *Sikh* and *Zulu* had arrived offshore. They, too, had navigation difficulties and began disembarking the Marines two miles west of the designated beach. High seas also proved to be rather much for the lighters which were being used to get the Marines ashore and some broke up. *Sikh* was now hit by shore batteries and suffered heavy casualties and *Zulu* had to take her under tow. Only 70 Marines were therefore landed and attempted to fight their way into the town, but were soon overwhelmed. Force B now tried to fight their way out, but almost all were killed, including Haselden, or captured, including Campbell and Swinburn. Indeed, only Langton and four others eventually reached safety.

Of the other raids in this series, only the LRDG's attack on Barce airfield was successful. Sixteen aircraft were destroyed and seven damaged for a loss of ten men captured and 14 vehicles destroyed. The Sudan Defence Force managed to gain a lodgement at Jalo, but the Italian defenders were too well prepared and after four days' bombardment of each other's positions the Sudan Defence Force were ordered to return to Kufra. Stirling failed to get to Benghazi harbour, being beaten back on the outskirts of the town by a garrison which was expecting the raid and he had a long and difficult journey back to Kufra, constantly harried by aircraft during the first part of the trip. Yet, for the LRDG and SAS these were only temporary setbacks. For 1 SS Regiment, on the other hand, and the SIG, *Agreement* marked their death knell.

The SIG had now been totally destroyed, while 1 SS Regiment was almost a skeleton of its former self. Little now remained of D Squadron and A Squadron had been taken over by the LRDG. B and C Squadrons were once more back under SOE control and continuing their training for their possible roles in the event of the Germans occupying Turkey and Syria. The failure of the German drive into the Caucasus during the summer of 1942 followed towards the end of the year by the debacle at Stalingrad, however, made this an increasingly unlikely option and instead the personnel of the two squadrons were used for SOE operations in the Balkans, losing their identity as 1 SS Regiment. Indeed, as far as GHQ MEF were concerned, by mid-January 1943 1 SS Regiment no longer existed in the order of battle.

As for the rationalisation of Special Forces in the Middle East, the concept of bringing them under one umbrella did come to some fruition in early 1943. This was not so much as a result of the discussions at GHQ MEF in the late summer of 1942, but more because David Stirling himself was captured by the Germans at the end of January 1943 during an operation in Tunisia. The upshot of this was that the SAS was retitled the Special Raiding Squadron

(SRS) and the SBS, now under Jellicoe's command, became the Special Boat Squadron, as opposed to No 1 Special Boat Section.

Both, together with the Greek Sacred Heart Squadron, were placed under Raiding Forces Middle East and brought in to command this organisation was none other than Kid Cator. He remained in command until after the Sicily landings, in which the SRS under Paddy Mayne and No. 3 Commando, which had come out from Britain and had also been placed under his command, played a distinguished part. This organisation was then broken up, partly because Laycock was now back in the Mediterranean as commander of the SS (Commando) brigade there and Cator's post quickly became superfluous, but also because the two men did not get on personally.

Raiding Forces Middle East was, however, resurrected in the autumn of 1943 under Brigadier Turnbull who now had the Sacred Heart Squadron, LRDG and SBS, with whom Ian Lapraik became a leading light, and later the Raiding Support Regiment. They were to operate until the end of the war in the Aegean, Adriatic, Balkans and Italy. As for Cator, he returned to England and became ADC to General Boy Browning, commander I Allied Airborne Corps. As such he took part in the great Allied airborne operation of September 1944, *Market-Garden*, and then retired to run his farm, his father having died.

Apart from Cator, the last of the original ME Commandos to remain in the Commando 'business' were some of his original Palestinians in No. 51 ME Commando. Those who had not been killed or captured while serving with the SIG or D Squadron 1 SS Regiment had returned to the AMPC. It so happened that No. 2 Commando, then serving in Italy and much reduced in strength after some four months' fighting, was given special permission to make good its losses from volunteers from the Mediterranean and Middle East theatres. GHQ MEF would only allow them, however, to recruit from among the ranks of the AMPC and it was from here that a number of former No. 51 members returned to the Commando fold and fought in the ranks of No. 2 Commando for the remainder of the war in Italy, the Adriatic and Balkans.

One of these who deserves particular mention is Zvi Zwet, who became No. 2's semi-official photographer, taking a number of very spectacular photographs until tragically losing both his legs on a Teller mine in April 1945 during the fighting on Lake Commacchio in northern Italy. Now distinguished in many fields in his own country of Israel, he remains a stalwart member of the Commando Association and is often in London to attend its functions.

The reconstituted Middle East Commando, about which

Churchill had been so emphatic, never had the *esprit de corps* and cohesion of its forbears. Formed from remnants of a variety of Special Forces units, all with disparate operational experiences, subjected to frequent changes of role and channels of command and control and diluted by transfers to such as the LRDG and SAS, it is hardly surprising that this was so. Even where former ME Commandos tried to foster the original spirit of *modus operandi* of 1940–41, they were to find that circumstances conspired against them, as we shall see in the next chapter.

CHAPTER SIX

Mission 204

Mission 204[1] was set up to provide aid to Chiang Kai Shek in his fight against the Japanese. The groundwork for it was laid in Burma as early as spring 1939 when it was decided to earmark suitable personnel who could help train Chinese guerrillas. A defence conference held in Singapore that summer confirmed the requirement but agreed that the mission would only be deployed if Britain found herself at war with Japan. Planning nevertheless continued.

In early 1941 Major General L.E. Denys MC was appointed Military Attaché at the British Embassy Chungking, Chiang Kai Shek's seat of government. The British were mindful that the Chinese were receiving increasing aid from the Americans, both unofficially in that Roosevelt allowed them to recruit pilots from the US Navy and the Army to form a force which would become known as Chennault's Flying Tigers, and also after March 1941, when the Lend-Lease Act was passed, officially in the shape of munitions. It was also accepted that should Burma be invaded support from the Chinese to the north could make a significant contribution to its defence. General Denys was therefore instructed to open talks with Chiang Kai Shek and to propose to him that Mission 204 be sent to China to provide guerrilla expertise in the form of squads who would be attached to Chinese guerrilla groups and as a clearing house for British munitions supplied to the Chinese. The Chinese premier proved to be very receptive and, apart from specialist instructors, it was decided that 15 squads should be raised and sent.

The original intention had been to select Chinese linguists, but there were few of these available. It was therefore decided to make the qualifications less stringent and to throw the net wider. The Australians agreed to furnish some squads and in early May 1941 Wavell, as C-in-C Middle East, was asked whether he had any suitable individuals whom he could spare. He replied by signal to the War Office, copied to the C-in-C Far East, on 16 May. He was primarily looking for personnel who had had experience with irregular forces in Abyssinia. (It should be remembered that Addis Ababa had fallen almost six weeks before, Amba Alagi had just been captured and all that remained was to hunt down the remnants of the

Italian presence.) Failing this, he wondered whether the Middle East Commandos and 'Layforce battalions' might be suitable. Although they had no experience of irregular forces 'they do contain officers and men prepared for rough stuff'.[1]

While it was perfectly understandable for Wavell to look towards the members of Mission 101 since their services were no longer needed so urgently in Abyssinia, it is significant that he should offer up Layforce and is indicative that he probably considered that, pressured as he was by the overall strategic situation of the time, that it was difficult to employ more than a portion in their true role and that they were an expensive luxury. Rather, though, than disband them and return their members to more conventional soldiering, which would have a grievous affect on morale, Mission 204 seemed an ideal way round the problem. C-in-C Far East replied next day that both were acceptable and tasked Wavell with the finding of three 'area officers', who would each control groups of guerrillas and seven squads, comprising in total seven officers (captain and below),

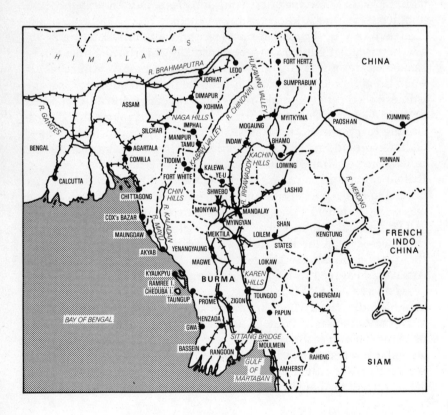

seven warrant officers, seven sergeants, seven corporals and 100 junior ranks. In addition he required some 20 signallers.

Shortly after this the Crete crisis arose which delayed Wavell from addressing the matter any further. On 25 June, having decided that Layforce should be disbanded, he informed the War office that one of the options open to its members was to 'volunteer for guerrilla activities in the Far East'. Eventually Wavell was able to raise a total of ten officers and 125 other ranks from Layforce and Mission 101 members.

Two officers were required to report to HQ Burma Command as soon as possible. It was thus that John Milman found himself boarding an Imperial Airways flying boat in the company of one of the more colourful characters of Mission 101, Major Count Arthur Bentinck DSO, a Coldstream Guardsman and 57-year-old veteran of the First World War, who had spent some months operating with the Abyssinians in the Lake Tana area and had earlier, during the Italo-Abyssinian war, served with an ambulance unit. They reported to HQ Burma Command in Rangoon and it was only then that they learnt what their role was to be.

The plan was to raise five Chinese guerrilla battalions, each 850 men strong, to operate in widely scattered key areas in China and be focal points of resistance against the Japanese. Each battalion would have attached to it three Mission 204 squads. A squad was to be made up of one officer and 15 other ranks, together with a Chinese-speaking liaison officer, and the three would be controlled by a headquarters run by an 'area officer'. It was, however, emphasised that the squads were not there to command the Chinese, but to act as advisers.

The Middle East contingent was to be divided into two groups, supporting two guerrilla battalions, while the other squads were to be found by the Australians and a contingent from Hong Kong and Malaya. John Milman was to command one Middle East group, while another Mission 101 veteran, Courtenay Brocklehurst, took over the other. Bentinck was given part of the Malayan contingent when it arrived.

The main body had gone by sea from Suez to Colombo and then on to India. Here they entrained for a journey across India to Calcutta and from there took another boat to Rangoon, eventually arriving there in early September. Up until now the concentration of Mission 204 had been conducted in great secrecy, but the day after the arrival of the Middle East contingent at Rangoon Tokyo radio broadcasted the fact. By the end of the month all squads had arrived and had concentrated at the euphemistically named Bush Warfare School at Maymyo, 30 miles east of Mandalay. Whether the title of the school had anything to do with the fact that part of its purpose was to convert the Middle East contingent from bush to jungle warfare must remain a matter for conjecture.

The school was commanded by a Paul Meade of the Frontier Force Rifles, whose experience was largely confined to the barren and treeless landscape of the North-West Frontier Province of India. His chief instructor, however, was a Sapper, Michael Calvert, who knew China and had seen the way the Japanese operated there. He had also fought in the ill-fated Norwegian campaign and had been involved with the training of special forces in Britain. Later he would become one of the leading lights of the Chindits.

When Milman and Bentinck had first arrived at Maymyo Calvert was away in Australia, organising commando and demolition training, and the task of drawing up a training programme was left initially to John Milman. He organised it essentially on commando lines, but with greater emphasis on explosives and booby-trap training. It was also necessary to acclimatise people to working with partisans and every man underwent a crash course in Chinese. Many exercises were organised and one of the more climactic involved the capture and simulated demolition of the huge bridge which spanned the Irrawaddy at Mandalay. The original intention had been to send reconnaissance parties, dressed in civilian clothes, into China in order to make contact with the Chinese and inspect the selected operational areas. This was abandoned, however, for fear of exciting Japanese hostility.

The Japanese attack on Pearl Harbor on 7 December 1941 caught Mission 204 while it was still training at Maymyo and was to mark a radical change in the fortune and destiny of the two Middle East contingents. The defence of Burma now became the overriding priority. To this end the two contingents were detached from Mission 204 and redesignated Special Service Detachments (SSD) 1 and 2. They were placed directly under the command of Burma Army.

This precipitated a desperate scramble to bring the detachments up to scale both in equipment and specialist personnel, especially medical. To the latter end John Milman managed to acquire the services of the leading military surgeon in Burma, Eric Parry, for SSD 1, but the medical staff directorate quickly woke up to this and replaced him with another, Dr McLane, who was to play a major part in seeing the detachment through the trials ahead and was to be recommended by Milman for the OBE. He also managed to get hold of a Burma resident, Beaver Barton, who had spent much time wandering about uncharted areas of the Burma-China border disguised as a Roman Catholic priest. It is perhaps indicative of the atmosphere of the time that there was a succession of signals between Rangoon and Delhi as to whether he should be allowed to keep his beard!

In early January 1942 SSD 1 was deployed to Loimwe in the eastern Shan States and was placed under command of Major General J.B. Scott's 1st Burma Division. This was holding a defensive line on the River Salween since it was believed that the Japanese would invade Burma from northern Thailand making use of the road that ran east-west, south of Mandalay, from Kengtung to Meiktila. As it happened the Japanese ruled this out because it meant a very long approach march through very mountainous country and opted instead to enter Burma much further south, a more direct route, even though it meant a 200-mile march through roadless jungle. Be that as it may, SSD 1's task was to deploy on the arc of a circle some 50 miles east of the Salween and harass the Japanese line of communication from advanced bases set up along its flank. The problem was that this took no account of the fact that the detachment was on its own, without the Chinese guerrilla battalion that it was supposed to support.

Luckily, before this plan could be implemented the area was taken over by elements of the Chinese Sixth Army. Chiang Kai Shek was concerned that the Japanese invasion of Burma might cut off his Lend–Lease supplies which were coming at that stage through the port of Rangoon and it was therefore in his interest to help defend the country. SSD 1 remained in the Loimwe area, but employed on quasi-engineering tasks – preparing the numerous road culverts for demolitions and booby-traps. They were still nominally under the command of 1st Burma Division, but their only means of communication was the Burma Posts and Telegraph, which was not wholly reliable. To keep itself supplied SSD 1 was reliant on dumps left by 1st Burma Division and local purchase. Since it was armed with Chinese Mannlicher rifles ammunition could be drawn from the Chinese and to this end William Seymour set up a small rear HQ next door to the Chinese HQ in Kengtung, the most easterly town in the Shan state of that name. By now it was clear that the Japanese were concentrating their efforts to the south of Rangoon and it seemed that SSD 1 was being left out on a limb. Communications with 1st Burma Division had broken down and when William

Seymour went to investigate he discovered that 1st Burma Division had moved out some days before without informing SSD 1.

Accordingly John Milman went to Army headquarters, now at Maymyo, to try and obtain some orders. Here he met the Chief of Staff, General Hutton, who told him to wait. At this stage there was a dramatic new twist to events. Milman was informed by Hutton that he was to come under command of Orde Wingate who had newly arrived in Burma.

Wingate had first earned his reputation as an expert in irregular warfare with his somewhat controversial involvement with the Jewish Night Squads during the Arab revolt in Palestine 1936–39. It was, however, his doings in Abyssinia that really caught the public eye. Here, as a member of Mission 101, he had led a band of Abyssinian irregulars known as Gideon Force and had accompanied the Emperor on his march to Addis Ababa. He had, though, fallen out with Sandford and was bitterly resentful of the seeming lack of recognition by General Platt of his efforts. Always vulnerable to mental depression, he had returned to Cairo and in July 1941 had attempted to commit suicide and dropped temporarily out of sight.

One man, however, had remembered him. This was Wavell who had been given the unenviable task of trying to coordinate Allied efforts – American, British, Dutch, Australian – to stem the Japanese onrush in South–East Asia. In his new capacity as C-in-C South West Pacific he asked for Wingate's services in a signal dated 6 February 1942. Initially he wanted him to act as a Brigadier General Staff to coordinate the efforts of the Chinese Fifth and Sixth Armies whom he expected to be moved into Burma complete. Wavell's original signal had been addressed to East African command under the assumption that Wingate was still employed by them. The War Office, too, seems to have been confused over his whereabouts and it was not until Auchinleck, still C-in-C Middle East, sent a somewhat stiff signal to the War Office on 15 February that the picture became clear. Wingate, the signal stated, had been sent back to Britain in September 1941 having been downgraded medically for six months. He was located and sent post haste to the Far East.

In the meantime, Chiang Kai Shek, partly because of Wavell's hesitancy in accepting two complete Chinese armies in Burma, insisted that they should be placed under command of the recently arrived General 'Vinegar Joe' Stilwell, whom Roosevelt had appointed Commanding General US Army Forces China-Burma-India theatre. Wavell, in view of Wingate's experience, now decided to use him to coordinate irregular warfare in Burma in the hope that this might help to slow down the Japanese advance. Milman was told by Hutton that he and Brocklehurst were to come under Wingate's command. Wingate now had a discussion with Milman and began to expound on his concept of deep penetration, drawing on his experience in Abyssinia.

Much of what Wingate said was not new to Milman since it was little more than the basic concepts in which the Middle East Commandos had been trained. But Wingate's attempt to compare Burma with Abyssinia was totally unrealistic in Milman's eyes. Abyssinia had a sparse but generally friendly population and the enemy was not of the same calibre as the Japanese were proving to be. Burma was more densely populated and the people were generally at best neutral.

Be that as it may, Wingate now handed Milman a written order. This was dated 29 March 1942 and headed 'Burma Army Long Range Penetration Group'. It stated that Wingate's intention was to concentrate all SSDs 'in the course of the coming fortnight at Corps HQ, at Allanmyo or wherever it may be'. Milman himself was ordered to move to Corps HQ 'with the minimum of delay' and report there 'complete with your unit and not less than 60 per cent of your total equipment and stores not later than 13/4/42'.

Milman reckoned that it would take all this time and even more to collect his widely dispersed unit and move it back. On 6 April Milman received a further signal from Wingate cancelling his previous orders and instructing SSD 1 to concentrate at Kengtung and await further orders. By the 10th this had been done and a week later came orders to move to Taungye. Before this Milman had sent Jocelyn Nicholls and his No. 2 Squad to the Salween to destroy the bridge carrying the Kengtung–Meiktila road over it and to provide demolition support to the Chinese. The Chinese commander assured John Milman that his intention was to hold where he was until the last man. Reassured by this, Milman went to visit Nicholls and found that the bridge and other installations had been destroyed. Milman therefore ordered him to return to base within 48 hours and returned to Kengtung to discover that in the meantime the Chinese had evacuated the area.

SSD 1 was now on its own, but two days later came more bad tidings when No 2 Squad returned with the news that they had been caught on the road by a Zero fighter and that Jocelyn Nicholls had been killed. By now SSD 1 was in very real danger of being cut off. There were two options, to head for Lashio, the railhead for the Burma Road into China, the main supply route for Lend–Lease, or to march to Kunming in Yunnan. Milman chose the former and sent William Seymour on ahead as a 'trailblazer'. No sooner had he done this than news came through that the Japanese were in Lashio, therefore Kunming it had to be. Luckily, Seymour also picked up this news and, on his own initiative, made for Kunming.

It took six weeks' march to reach Kunming. The route consisted of mule and coolie tracks, as well as crossing the Mekong river. SSD 1 managed to obtain the services of a Chinese mule contractor and his mules to carry their rations and heavy equipment. Fifty, with their handlers, absconded on the first night, and the Commandos took over the other 50 themselves. Only five survived the march. Luckily the party had sufficient hard rations to see them through, albeit on short commons, and only one died, of dysentery. During the last stage they were a little delayed by bickering between the Yunnanese Army and Chiang Kai Shek's central government troops. This manifested itself in innumerable road blocks manned by Chiang Kai Shek's men. Eventually they reached Kunming on 9 July. William Seymour was there to greet them with some lorries which took them to a YMCA camp. They were, however, delayed in entering the camp for a couple of hours because of shooting between Chiang Kai Shek's men and the Yunnanese troops. They remained at the YMCA camp for two weeks recovering from the march.

During this time John Milman flew to Chungking and reported to HQ Mission 204. General Denys had been killed in an air crash in March and the mission was now commanded by Major-General J.M. Bruce. Bruce told him of the adventures of the Australian and Malayan contingents of the mission, who had eventually got into China. It also transpired that a recent visitor had been Wingate who had proposed that he take over Mission 204, a suggestion which did not go down well.

In late July SSD 1 were flown back to India. They staged at an airfield in Upper Assam and were joined by a survivor of SSD 2, Raider Cornec. Brocklehurst's group had originally been deployed to west of the Salween and had then decided to get back to India. They had managed to cross the upper part of the Irrawaddy plain in one body, but thereafter, faced with dense jungle, they had been forced to split up into small groups. Most of these were lost in the jungle and never heard of again, although one party was taken in by a friendly hill village and eventually rescued from there. One group of 15, with Beaver Barton and an officer called Davidson-Houston, fell in with Stilwell at the beginning of May and accompanied him on his march out of Burma.

On arrival in Calcutta towards the end of July 1942 SSD 1 was sent on leave. Milman was summoned to Delhi for a personal interview with Wavell, whose interest in SSD 1 stemmed as much as anything from its Middle East Commando origins. Wavell asked Milman whether he would like to join Wingate, but the offer was politely declined. The Commander-in-Chief also handed him a personal handwritten letter to be read out to the detachment:

> Will you please let the officers and men of the 1st Special Service Detachment know how much I appreciate what they have done and the stout heart and spirit with which they have met dangers, hardships and disappointments. I hope that they will now have a period of rest, after which they will, with their invaluable training and experience, be of the greatest use in future operations and in training others.

After leave the detachment reassembled at Deolali and, with no role left for it it was disbanded.

It is clear that without their Middle East Commando background the members of SSD 1 would have been hard put to survive the rigours and frustrations of Burma 1942 and that their shared experience of this welded them even more closely together. Unfortunately, Wingate was now seen as the man of the hour and the fact that Milman and his men had a much more realistic idea of what Special Forces could achieve in the jungle was disregarded. Perhaps, above all, the lesson learnt by No. 52 ME Commando in southern Sudan and Abyssinia that long range penetration of the enemy's lines by large bodies of troops was counter-productive might have, if it had been heeded, meant the avoidance of the unacceptably high casualties suffered during the first Chindit expedition of 1943 with no lessening of the morale effect it had on the Allied forces in Burma and an even deeper impression on the Japanese.

CHAPTER SEVEN

Appraisal

As we have seen, by the end of 1942 the Middle East Commandos had vanished. Those of their members who were not dead or languishing in prisoner of war camps had joined other units and organisations and had quickly cemented new loyalties. It was thus understandable that the majority would put their service in the ME Commandos into the back of their minds, especially since this period of service took place in the darkest period of the war and they would prefer to remember the years of victory which followed. Those who had been prisoners wanted to forget what they had been through and put their priority into picking up the threads of their lives once more.

In 1946, the Army Commandos were disbanded and the Commando responsibility was passed over to the Royal Marines, who had begun to form their own Commandos in 1942. This reduced the Commando link still further and, as far as the Army Commandos themselves were concerned, it was only through the Commando Association that their spirit endured. This had been formed in 1943 by Colonel Charles Vaughan, commandant of the Commando Basic Training Centre at Achnacarry in Scotland. This, of course, was long after the disbandment of the Middle East Commandos and it was natural that almost all its members came from the UK-based Commandos among whom there was a determined drive to ensure that everyone joined. Indeed, most former Middle East Commandos, on their return from the war, were either not aware of its existence or, if they had continued in the Commando business, joined on the basis of their later Commando affiliations.

Matters were not helped by the publication of Hilary St George Saunders' *The Green Beret* in 1949. Since he had been the official Recorder at Combined Operations Headquarters in England, his book was as definitive as could be, given the obvious security restrictions, especially so soon after the war. Unfortunately, nowhere in the book was any mention made of the Middle East Commandos. Until the official wartime papers on the Commandos began to be released to the Public Record Office from 1970 onwards, no other real attempt was made to revise the history and by that stage only those who had served in them were aware that the Middle

East Commandos had existed. Even then, the records proved to be very incomplete. While War Diaries do exist for No. 52 ME Commando and D Battalion Layforce, there are none for No. 50 and only one for No. 51, covering its first three months before it went to East Africa. References are made in other War Diaries, especially that of G(R) Branch, and in a few GHQ MEF files dealing with Special Forces. Without some background knowledge, it was difficult for researchers to find these.

Another difficulty was over the granting of Battle Honours to the Commando Association in 1957. The Association's Battle Honours committee contained no ME Commando representative, simply because there were hardly any ME Commando members in the Association at that time. Thus the Association applied for Honours affecting only the UK-based Commandos, and the only two covering the Middle East were Crete, which was applied for on behalf of No. 7 Commando, and the two blanket Honours of Middle East 1941, 1942, 1944 (No. 7 on Crete, No. 5 on Madagascar and 2 Special Service Brigade in the Adriatic) and North Africa 1941–43, which covered the operations of the UK-raised elements of Layforce in 1941 and Nos 1 and 6 Commandos in the Torch landings and subsequently Tunisia. The part played by Nos 51 and 52 ME Commandos in Sudan, Eritrea and Abyssinia received no recognition, and neither did the operations of Nos. 50 and 51 in North Africa in late 1940, although of course, they were largely abortive, but not through any fault of the ME Commandos.

In 1985, George Young, on behalf of the Middle East Commando Historical Research Group, took the matter of the East Africa Battle Honours up with the Commando Association, who in turn applied to the Ministry of Defence. The Honours claimed were Keren and Amba Alagi on behalf of No. 51 ME Commando and Abyssinia 1940–41, which includes the fighting in Sudan and Eritrea, for both Nos. 51 and 52. A reply was eventually received from the Ministry of Defence in the late summer of 1986. It stated that awarding of Battle Honours 'more than 40 years after the event' would be 'most unusual', perhaps forgetting that that of Namur was not granted until 1909, 214 years after the siege had taken place. It then went on to remind the Commando Association of the letter written by Field Marshal Sir Gerald Templer, the CIGS in 1957, to Colonels of Regiments:

I would ask you to give this matter your earnest personal attention and to see that only those battles and campaigns claimed as Honours which

bring to the mind and memory of your Regiment some service beyond
the call of duty.

The Ministry of Defence used this argument to refute the claims for
Keren and Amba Alagi on the grounds that 'albeit important' the
Commandos' roles had been 'largely patrolling and flanking
operations'. While appreciating the disappointment that rejection of
the application for these Battle Honours would bring to the former
ME Commandos, the letter went on to say that 'it has to be accepted
that the Battle Honours awarded to your Association in 1957 were
given in recognition of the service by Commando units in the Middle
East including the Abyssinian campaign'.[1] This reveals a surprising
ignorance by the Honours and Distinctions Committee for the Army
in that the Battle Honour Middle East 1941–44 does not cover the
campaigns in Eritrea and Abyssinia. Thus, while the reasons for not
granting Keren and Amba Alagi can perhaps be accepted, although
No. 51's performance at Amba Alagi did make an important
contribution to victory, there are no grounds for rejecting Abyssinia
1940–41, to which the Commando Association, through the
presence in Eritrea of both Nos. 51 and 52 and in Abyssinia of No. 51,
must still remain entitled.

The Middle East Commandos were formed in 1940 in response to
a demand from the Prime Minister. Unfortunately, it was not
realised by GHQ MEF at the time that the three ME Commandos
would put an increased strain on the already very stretched
resources of the theatre. Thus, while there was no problem in finding
sufficient volunteers, equipment was hard to come by and the lack of
it was to restrict the Commandos operationally, especially on
Castelorizzo and Crete, and in Abyssinia.

In the beginning, the planning for the early raiding operations on
the North African coast was realistic and coordination between the
Army and Navy good. Unfortunately, once the three ME
Commandos became dispersed both planning and appreciation of
their limitations deteriorated. Castelorizzo was a classic example of
this, with No. 50 only being properly briefed on the operation when
they were at sea and having only the very sketchiest intelligence
made available to them.

By the beginning of 1941 Wavell's slender forces were being
committed to an increasing number of different simultaneous
campaigns. It was thus probably inevitable that the ME
Commandos' specialist role should be forgotten and that they should
be regarded merely as a reserve of manpower. This was the reason

why No. 52 and then No. 51 were sent to help clear the Italians from East Africa and Abyssinia. It was lack of unit transport which prevented No. 52 from taking part in the follow up of the Italian withdrawal through Eritrea and No. 51, as well, had problems in this respect, especially in terms of resupply in front of Keren. True, the formation commanders did try to make use of ME Commandos' specialist skills, but they were not equipped for prolonged operations. Indeed, in spite of the equipment shortfalls, it is remarkable what No. 51 were able to achieve in Eritrea and Abyssinia.

Crete brought out the penalty of not providing the Commandos with support weapons – mortars and heavy machine guns. In spite of this, D Battalion (No. 50/52) Layforce did all that was asked of it as the major part of the rearguard and it was the sacrifice made on the island by the Middle East Commandos, A Battalion of Layforce and the Australian and Maori elements, who fought alongside them, which enabled as many men as there were to be evacuated. The need for integral heavy weapons was a lesson which took a long time to be assimilated. It was not until after it had been reinforced by the experience of Nos. 1 and 6 Commandos in Tunisia that a Heavy Weapons troop was incorporated in each Commando in time for the landings on Sicily in July 1943.

Given the grim situation in the Middle East after the loss of Crete, it is not surprising that Wavell and then Auchinleck wanted to disband the Commandos in the theatre. Manpower was at a premium. Apart from No. 51 still in Abyssinia, there was little left of the Middle East Commandos. C Battalion Layforce had lost heavily in the Litani River landing and only B Battalion was intact, although part of it was besieged in Tobruk.

Churchill's demand that the Commandos in the Middle East be resurrected resulted in the reformed Middle East Commando, but it was to be of a very different character to its predecessors. For a start, it contained a polygot mixture of ME Commandos, David Stirling's fledgling SAS and the Special Boat Service, all of whom had widely differing specialist roles. The SAS and the SBS soon left the ME Commando fold, and the rump of the ME Commando passed to under control of SOE Middle East and Balkans.

Confusion, however, still reigned, with GHQ MEF's efforts to bring Popski's Private Army under the Commando fold, together with its proposals to raise Afridi and Indian Commando units. The formation of the Special Interrogation Group merely served to compound this. The change of title to 1st Special Service Regiment in May 1942 was in an effort to rationalise the situation and reaffirm the ties of the unit to SOE. This was almost immediately negated by Rommel's new offensive in the Western Desert, which resulted in the squadrons of 1 SS Regiment being drawn in to defend Cairo. Thereafter, in spite of SOE objections, the operational control of 1 SS Regiment was usurped by Eighth Army. Part was lost in the abortive raid on Tobruk in September 1942, as we have seen, one squadron was absorbed by the LRDG, leaving SOE with just two squadrons. By this stage, the last vestiges of the original Middle East Commandos had vanished.

The story of the Middle East Commandos has a number of lessons on the use of Special Forces which are as relevant today as they ever were. Indeed, the plethora of 'private armies' in the Middle East during 1941–42 demonstrates only too clearly what can happen if there is lack of control and coordination in the higher echelons of command. Special Forces must not be raised unless the role for them has been properly defined beforehand. Organisation and equipment must be properly tailored to the role, and if the latter is changed then both must be adapted to reflect this. There must be a clearcut chain of command and control should be exercised at the highest possible level of command. This is especially so with operations involving more than one service. Planning must involve the Special Forces themselves; they should not be called upon to carry out operations on which they have had no opportunity to proffer advice.

Much of the British use of Special Forces during the Second World War was highly successful, but there is a natural tendency to remember just the successes and not the failures. The Middle East Commandos were victims of the circumstances outside their own control. In view of the difficulties and frustrations under which they laboured, it is remarkable what they were able to achieve. Compared to their UK-based counterparts, their efforts have gone too long unrecognised. If this book will have achieved nothing else, it will at least set the record straight.

Typical Middle East Commando Outline Initial Training Programme

(from War Diary G(R) Branch GHQ MEF, PRO WO 169/20)

1st Week: Map reading and compass work
Stalking and use of cover
Knotting, lashing and demolitions (officers and section commanders only)
24 hours scheme
Lectures on night work and stalking

2nd Week: Map reading and compass work
Camel riding, rowing and swimming
Knotting, lashing and demolitions
36 hours scheme – desert country
Lectures – guerrilla tactics and First Aid

3rd Week: Weapon training – rifle and revolver
Compass marching and stalking
Camel riding and rowing
48 hours scheme – bush country
Lectures – First Aid

4th Week: Weapon training – rifle and revolver
Bridging expedients
Camel riding and rowing
48 hours scheme – crossing water obstacles

5th Week: Weapon training – grenades and demolitions (night and day)
Rowing and boatwork
48 hours scheme – landing from ships' boats

6th Week: Weapon training – Fanny, bayonet, Tommy gun and machine pistol
Method of attacking specific targets
48 hours scheme – night rowing, landing, crossing, obstacles

PT was carried out each day when in camp.

APPENDIX II

Report of Landing of No. 50 Commando in Castelrosso [sic] Island, Italian Dodecanese

(Written by Major S.M. Rose, Second-in-Command No. 50 ME Commando, a few days after the operation, 25–28 Feb 1941)

After we had transshipped at SUDA to the two destroyers we had one rowing practice after dark and after that were soon at sea. We had very reasonable weather. This was lucky, for sea-sickness can bring a landing force to a state of complete uselessness. Our course was an indirect one towards the Palestine coast, turning N.E. in the late afternoon so as to arrive at the objective on the second night at 0300 hrs. We were escorted by the 2nd. [sic–3rd] Cruiser Squadron which was to cover us throughout the operation. Their particular duty was to prevent any naval interference from RHODES, which was 60 miles from CASTELROSSO to the N.W. We were by now old friends of the DECOY and HEREWARD as these same ships had so nearly landed us at BOMBA, and we had visited them several times at ALEXANDRIA and SUDA BAY. We brought the men on deck at their boat stations one hour before the time of landing to get their eyes used to the dark.

A British submarine showed us a light off the S.W. point of the island at about 0230 hrs., and after some very careful navigation amongst small rock islands, we arrived at the place for the landing at 0330 hrs. about 200 yds. off shore. At first everything went according to plan and the first flight were away with the second flight standing by ready to move aft from the mess deck. The boats were a very long time in returning and had been away for nearly an hour when we heard several bursts of machine gun fire and some single shots. We all thought this was the first encounter with the enemy post on NIFTIS POINT, close to where the landing was to take place, and expected searchlights and coastal batteries to pick us up at any moment. After this firing there was silence but still no boats returning. We then heard some firing, which was unmistakably a tommy gun. A whaler came alongside followed by a second one, but on inspection in the dim light we could see that they were still full of men of the first flight. Lt. Q. (R.N.R.) who was attached to the Commando, said that the whole of the first flight, except for these two boats, had passed the landing point and had rowed straight into the town harbour and had been machine-gunned by the sentries. As these two boats became separated they decided to return to the ships. All the time it was becoming lighter and it would be another half hour before daylight. Both destroyers began hoisting boats as quickly as possible as the landing had lost surprise now, and the senior ship had signalled to withdraw. The boats returned one by one round the point and seemed terribly slow returning. We expected that we might not be able to wait for the last two boats as it was now almost daylight. At last they appeared with only their crews aboard, which was puzzling, but at the same time we received a message from the Senior Naval Officer that the landing was now to proceed according to plan. The first flight rowed ashore in full daylight, followed by the second flight. There was no opposition at the landing beach, but there was intermittent firing going on in the town, about a mile distant. Just as it was getting light, H.M.S. LADYBIRD appeared from the straits between the island and the Turkish coast. She steamed straight into the harbour and opened up with her multiple pom-pom and 6″ gun at the PALEOCASTRO FORT where the Italian garrison had withdrawn to. One company occupied the important buildings in the town where there was little fighting except for the despatching of one or two sentries. The CARABINIERI station, wireless station, Governor's house and offices were occupied. Another company attacked the FORT, aided by covering fire from the LADYBIRD. The remaining half company climbed the heights to the flank of the fort to prevent the enemy escaping to the hills in the centre of the island. The fort fell at about 1000 hrs. and the small Italian garrison put up a very brave fight. They numbered about 50 armed men not all of them soldiers. There were customs guards, police, marines and a few airmen and soldiers. There were two officers.

Soon after dawn four C.R. 42 fighters came over, followed later by some S.81 or 79 tri-motor bombers. They bombed the slopes leading up to the Fort, and scored a hit on the LADYBIRD, which had to leave at once and re-embark the marines she had landed. Bombing and machine gunning went on all day. Although it was very frightening they did not cause any casualties.

Although the landing had been muddled the initial attack had been successful and we had captured the island with few casualties and very little opposition.

We collected up the prisoners, attended to all wounded, set up military control of the island and buried the dead.

During a very tiresome and noisy day we brought down two bombers into the sea and damaged a seaplane. The Italians tried to pick up the crew of a fallen bomber by landing a Red Cross seaplane alongside. Some long range bren shooting soon put a stop to this and put the seaplane out of action. The Turks later came out in a fishing boat to pick the air crew up.

The Turks had a dress circle view of all this as a small town lay facing us about three miles distant, across the straits.

The Naval Officer in charge of the landing boats had not read his chart properly and passed the landing beach and took the boats on another 1000 yds. right into the harbour: when they were fired at they turned about and went back to find the right place, but some boats became lost and had to return to the ships whilst others landed in the correct place. They met an Italian patrol shortly after landing, which was the cause of the tommy gun shooting. Two of them were killed and the remainder fled to the town leaving an excellent blood trail to be followed by all landing parties. As soon as it began to get dark the last sortie of bombers and fighters from RHODES returned home, leaving us with splitting headaches and singing ears. We had no casualties as most of their bombing was directed at the approaches to PALEOCASTRO FORT which had long been in our hands and had wisely been evacuated, except for a section. Headquarters were established in a disused sepulchre cut into the side of the cliff. As soon as it was dark, Headquarters moved into the town leaving two companies on the outskirts. Normal guards, pickets and patrols were detailed and the rest of the force got down to much needed rest.

With the disappearance of the last enemy bomber we thought that our troubles were ended until dawn the following morning. We only vaguely considered the possibilities of a sea borne counter attack, knowing that the record of the Italian Navy was one of avoiding battle, and knowing that we were covered by a Cruiser Squadron of the Royal Navy.

The headquarter staff slept in the governor's office with a sentry group outside. We were all very tired and slept well from 2000 hrs. We were awakened later at about 2100 hrs. by a very bright light. I thought that the enemy had dropped parachute flares and was about to bomb us out of the Governate. On looking through the window towards the open sea we were blinded by a searchlight beam which unmistakably came from a warship. From the time of being roused – the discovery of the cause of the bright light – to the firing of the first shell was all a matter of seconds. We were all on our feet crowding for the door, sentries, guard, batmen, Adjutant, M.O., Colonel, 2nd in command, G.II Staff Officer. Two shells had struck the building before we were all clear and several more followed as we leapt down the steps outside and dived for a narrow side street. Before gaining safety, some of us ran up a side street and inadvertently out on to a causeway into the beam of the searchlight. We quickly retraced our steps and dived for another turning. We then had some difficulty collecting up the unit headquarters in dark and narrow streets. Capt. B. and Lt. H. occupied the Governor's house and shared his double bed but were soon out of it when the shelling of the Governate started on the other side of the harbour. Meanwhile the ship was coming slowly into the harbour, shooting with her 4″ guns at all the important buildings, the monastery and fort. Major W. was sent at once to get in touch with our own warships. Looking round the corner of dark and narrow side streets where they joined the open and floodlit harbour, we could see the dark outline of the destroyer now only about 150 yards away, with her two searchlights groping about like long fingers trying to locate our troops. The noise and blast effect of this point blank range shelling was extremely frightening. It was no good shooting at the ship from the edge of the harbour as it would be inaccurate and probably ineffective, besides the reply would be a 4″ shell or pom-pom.

It was decided that in a fight with any landing force in narrow streets in the dark with an enemy who probably knew the geography of the town would be to our disadvantage and so one company and headquarters withdrew to the CEMETERY to cover the landing beach. The other company were on the other side of the harbour and we were at this time out of touch with them. The withdrawal from the town was unpleasant as we had to pass along an open causeway avoiding the searching beams from another ship. We spent the rest of the night expecting a landing and avoiding searchlights by lying behind rocks. It was extremely cold and rain made matters worse. During the night nobody knew quite who was who and we unfortunately killed one of our own men. Several of the prisoners escaped, one being intercepted by my batman and suitably dealt with.

At dawn we made prearranged signals at the landing beach to indicate that we were still in possession of the island and that it was safe for the relieving force in the transport, H.M.T. ROSAURA escorted by destroyers DECOY and HEREWARD to approach, land fresh troops and take the Commando away. Shortly before dawn, the Company Commander of the company which had been left on the other side of the town all night, came in to report and give an account of enemy activities after we had withdrawn from the town.

The destroyer that entered the harbour had landed about a platoon of sailors or marines armed with rifles and automatics. They then entered the Governate and ran round knocking at the doors of houses along the waterfront. Italian nationals came out of hiding and were taken to the ship using many small boats that were tied up in the harbour. They also landed a small number of men from an 'E' boat outside the harbour, but they were driven back by our men by rifle fire. During the night we had lost a few men from shelling, mostly the guards we had left on important buildings, all of which were shelled. Capt. B. also reported the town clear of enemy, and gave details of the time of their departure. This was most important news as we all thought that dawn would see a fight to re-capture the town against a fresh and better armed enemy with our own force divided and the two halves out of touch.

No ships arrived and therefore no relieving force. At first light an enemy reconnaissance bomber came over followed later by more bombers and fighters. The troops were a little puzzled when it was announced that the relieving force had failed to arrive and was not now likely to arrive until the following night or dawn the next morning. The day was spent organising food distribution to the starving civilian Greek population from Italian rations, exploring the island and rounding up some sailors who had run to the hills. The troops were very tired and all those not on duty, military or civil, rested.

The Governate had been hit by 4 or 5 shells, two entering the seaward wall of the room we were all sleeping in, leaving two gaping holes and a floor covered with brick and plaster. The shells had ploughed into the ceiling where they burst. I cannot understand why it was that no one was killed as at least one of these shells must have come in as we were leaving as several had cut faces from flying bricks. It also looked as if they had fired on seeing us at the window. The ships must have been within 300 yards when she first opened fire.

They had tried to move the Governor's safe but had found it too heavy. It would not have mattered much as we had already removed the cypher books and all documents of importance. The Governor was in our hands.

The second day was reasonably quiet. Bombing was less intense. The local inhabitants became quite out of hand and looted all the Italian houses for food and trinkets. We had to threaten them with shooting before they would see reason. The population of the town

was about 3000 with many empty and ruined houses. The island is
about 2 x 4 miles with a high plateau running close to the shore rising
to a maximum of 700 ft. On top of the plateau were a few farms and
some poor quality gravel fields. Water is obtained in cisterns from
concrete catchments. The population are almost entirely Greek with
a few Turks and Armenians. Our doctor told us that the people
showed the symptoms of undernourishment . They told us that they
had imported meat once a month, and when we used the bakery the
people crowded round to see the loaves, as if it were some puppet
show. No bread had been baked for a very long time. The troops were
very generous and on the first day gave tins of bully to what seemed
to be a starving population, little realising that we would be
desperately hungry ourselves before long.

The day closed with a great deal of cheering in the town. Now that
the Italian nationalists had gone they felt safe with a Union Jack over
the Governate and British troops occupying the island. The new
mayor and corporation were elected in place of the Quisling Greeks
who were now in disgrace and there was much business going on in
the Administrative Office in the town. Fascist signs were taken down
and the Mayor in his speech said that the people were pleased that in
future they would elect their own representatives and have some say
in the administration of the island. Greek flags were hoisted on all
caiques in the harbour. We had still no communication with our
ships. We had a good night's rest.

At dawn on the third day we made our signals again with no
results. This time the troops were becoming a little restive and the
'barrack room lawyers' were holding forth pessimistic theories,
which had to be suppressed at once by officers who overheard them.
The prospects were not too good as we had little food and not very
much ammunition if the enemy made a strong seaborne counter
attack. The bombers came over as usual, but seemed to know more
exactly where we were. One of the prisoners or civilians who were
evacuated had probably given a full description of our positions.

We discussed the possibilities of a counter attack, and thought
that on the whole, it was unlikely as it would take some time to
organise, and it ran the risk of being intercepted by our cruisers. A
warship crammed with troops cannot fight a battle.

Reconnaissance patrols were sent to various parts of the island to
watch beaches and give signals, and working parties were sent to the
fort to bring down some sacks of Italian biscuits, which we needed
badly. At 0900 hrs. on this third morning, we were warned by a
breathless runner that two destroyers had been sighted close into the

Turkish coast, heading in our direction. We had failed to see the
verey lights fired by a beach patrol against the bright sunlight.
Shortly after the arrival of the runner, two destroyers came round the
point close inshore. A naval officer, who was attached to us,
recognised them at once as Italian, although they flew no colours.
This was a most unexpected surprise and caught us quite
unprepared with men all over the place – patrols, fatigue parties,
men filling water bottles in the town, sentry posts in the town etc.
The enemy landed in the harbour and infiltrated along the causeway
towards the CEMETERY, and to the high ground up to the fort. Some
bren shooting made them extremely cautious but in return we had 4″
shells, Bredas and machine guns. This counter attack was supported
by many bombers dropping showers of anti-personnel 40 lb. bombs
and dive machine gunning from C.R. 42 fighters.

    The situation demanded considerable self control and personal
leadership from officers and N.C.Os. The battle was very intense
with enemy naval and air forces against us with little hope of
retaliation. At this stage the appearance of our destroyers and some
air arm fighters would have saved the day.

    At mid-day, the two isolated companies, one at the Cemetery and
one at the landing point were forced to withdraw to the top of the
cliff. This was not due to pressure from enemy ground troops, but to
consolidate our position on high ground, and avoid being overlooked
by the enemy, who were advancing along the top of the cliff. It also
cleared us from a very unhealthy spot so far as bombing was
concerned. This became more imperative when the enemy landed
men behind us at our landing beach covered by a destroyer. It was
lucky that the commanders of the various detachments all thought
alike and made for the same place, as there could be no signal
communications and a journey along the causeway meant certain
death to any runner. In the late afternoon two of our patrols joined us
on the top of the cliff. They had withdrawn from the FORT and
western beach where they had been when the counter attack started.
They had been extremely well led by their officers, who had inflicted
a good many casualties on the enemy struggling up a zig-zag path
towards the top of the cliff. Towards dusk the enemy occupied a ridge
about 1000 yards in front of us and stood on the skyline like a lot of
tourists, sightseeing – they then proceeded to advance with a few
sections forward, who were searching the rocks ahead of them. Their
advance was very sticky and we heard an N.C.O. shout 'Avante
NICOLO avante, avante' as he reprimanded one of his men for lack of
determination. When the leading troops presented a good target our

leading sections opened fire at about 300 yds. This was followed by a good deal of long range bren and machine gun shooting but there was little danger as the grey rocks afforded uncomfortable but excellent cover. As the sun went down the shooting ceased.

Before giving an account of the final withdrawal it is necessary to make an appreciation of the Commandos' position.

1. The force was still intact but had two officers and about 60 men missing.
2. Food and water were non-existent and the water points were in the hands of the enemy.
3. Apart from the ammunition carried by the men, our reserves were on the beach and were so far as we knew in the enemy's possession.
4. The morale of the force was somewhat shaken, and all were fatigued.
5. It was now clearly only a matter of time before we would be defeated unless help arrived.

It was obvious that the enemy were relying on cowing us with air bombing and shelling and would later advance and mop up their exhausted and frightened opponents. They had certainly succeeded in confining us to a very limited area with a 600 ft. precipice to our rear and flanks with only one narrow and difficult goat track down to the landing point. On the fourth morning they would certainly be able to inflict considerable casualties with their bombers, and during a lull could advance to finish us off. Fire from their ships would now be ineffective as the shells grazed the edge of the cliff but they could certainly prevent us from using the goat track.

We would of course wait to see if our ships would turn up that night or at dawn the next morning but beyond that we had four alternatives.

1. To make a final attack on the enemy in front of us and try to regain the town.
2. To withdraw to another part of the island on the plateau.
3. To surrender.
4. To stay where we were.

Alternative one could not meet with much success as the unit was disorganised and had little fight left in it. Two presented further water difficulties besides putting us further away from the pre-arranged landing point, where a relieving force might appear. Three was the most humiliating and unpleasant of all but certainly received consideration.

It was decided to wait until the early hours of the morning and to see what might turn up in the night. Those who had to make decisions were clearly suffering from fatigue. I think myself that dawn would have found us in the same position and we might conceivably have held out to the following night and perhaps longer. There was very little patrol activity on either side. Automatic fire was opened at what was thought to be an enemy patrol but it turned out to be our prisoners, under escort, coming from the rear. They had been pushed forward earlier in the evening to get them clear of Headquarters, who were at the top of the goat track. This was an unfortunate incident due to the escorts failing to be in front to answer the challenge, and due to the fact that they were in Italian uniforms and moved in file. Three or four were killed and others injured. The incident might have been difficult to explain had we later been captured. There was every evidence that the British had shot their prisoners.

At midnight, sentries reported that they could hear the crackling of steam pipes and the noise of turbines, peculiar to destroyers. It was different to the Italian destroyers which had cruised around all day. We had lost all our signalling kit, and at first matches then a pocket torch were used. There was no reply at first, but we were certain that they were our ships when we heard a rich flow of language from some petty officer giving orders about lowering boats.

I was sent down the goat track with an escort to get in touch with the senior Naval Officer commanding the destroyers. After a perilous descent in the dark, we signalled from the shore for a boat and went aboard the DECOY to give details of the situation on the island. The landing of the relieving force was cancelled and boats were sent in to evacuate the Commando. My party later re-landed to act as guides and organise the evacuation.

The Commandos withdrew in very moderate order, leaving quantities of arms and equipment behind. We managed to get all our wounded and about 12 prisoners off.

Strong naval forces had arrived. Cruisers, H.M.S. YORK, BONAVENTURE, GLOUCESTER, destroyers H.M.S. HERO, HERE-WARD, DECOY, JAGUAR. Some torpedoes were fired into the harbour but we never heard of the results. We were told later that one of our ships had let an Italian destroyer slip away unmolested through a misunderstanding.

It was a most incredible contrast to be on top of the cliff, parched with thirst, hunger and cold one moment, and a little later having a whiskey and soda in a comfortable wardroom. As soon as we were clear of the island the sea became extremely rough and remained so until we reached Suda Bay. A month's rations for one of the relieving companies and a great deal of ammunition were swept straight overboard, and several whalers were smashed. We were all terribly seasick, the wardroom becoming a complete shambles with groaning officers lying about the place. I was very sorry for our wounded. So ended the first Commando operation. '

HERAKLION, CRETE
3rd March 1941

Crete: Extracts from Layforce War Diary

(Written up by Capt. Evelyn Waugh)

27 May

0800: Enemy air activity began and continued with two brief lulls until dusk. In the forenoon it was mainly concentrated on hills to left flank of 'A' Bn's position. Throughout the day SPHAKION ROAD was thronged with retreating men who moved in independent groups, taking cover during attack and pushing on during intermissions.

Throughout day 'A' Bn held a line from road to foothills East of SUDA. 'D' Bn remained under cover in neighbourhood of SPHAKION roads near Bde HQ with orders to fall back at dusk (less det. one coy.) to positions further South. Det. one coy 'D' Bn with Maoris in support ordered to hold ascent at T road junction 208516 and road East of junction. This road to be cratered during night.

2100: At sunset Adv HQ (Bde Cmd and BM) proceeded to contact Bns. They met 'I' Tanks under cmd and ordered them to road North of STYLOS. Enemy reported on left flank, in consequence of which rear HQ moved to road.

2300: Lt Col COLVIN arrived at rear HQ reporting his line outflanked and in danger of being overrun. He ordered rear HQ to withdraw to Ay. EFSTRATIOS.

28 May

0600: Shortly after dawn Adv HQ made contact with part of 'A' Bn, N of STYLOS. This Bn had fallen back during the night through the det. 'D' Bn of whom no further news was gained. Fire was opened by enemy sub-machine gunners who were scattered by 'I' Tank. Det. 'A' Bn under Major WYLIE, in conjunction with some New Zealanders, counter attacked and drove enemy from position.

1000: In absence of orders Col. LAYCOCK held conference with two New Zealand and Australian Brigadiers. LAYFORCE now became merged into a single unit and the original plan of falling back through successive Bn positions was modified. LAYFORCE now fell back on line North of BABALI INN, which it held until darkness under heavy mortar bombing and sniping.

1200: Bde HQ last house in village of BABALI.

1500: Bde HQ moved to Ay. ANTONIOS.

After leaving BABALI enemy made little attempt to press retreating forces. Col. LAYCOCK's own appreciation of this was that they were indifferent to the fate of British troops in the island, but used them as a lure to draw ships into dive-bombing range. They therefore had no wish to prevent embarkation at beaches and from sunset 28 May barely kept touch.

2100: LAYFORCE withdrew from line of BABALI INN. In original rearguard plan force was now to have taken up position during darkness South of VRYSOS and dumps of amn. and rations were established here. Now, however, in view of the losses sustained and the exhaustion of the remaining troops, Major Gen. WESTON relieved bde of its rearguard role and ordered it to proceed to the assembly area South of IMVROS and East of SPHAKION at mouth of SPHAKION RAVINE covering right flank during evacuation.

2200: Bde passes through VRYSOS which was burned out and totally deserted. Here a det. RE were waiting to blow bridge after last vehicle. Although orders were given this bridge was never blown owing to failure of preparation.

2330: Bde HQ reached point on road near ALIKAMBOS where det. RE had blown road without orders and were engaged on repairing it. Here some MT was available which was sent back to lift marching troops as far as crater. Remaining rations were distributed. The last 'I' Tank was driven broadside across road, the water emptied and the engine left running.

29 May
0500: LAYFORCE reached IMVROS where were established Maj Gen WESTON's HQ and an ambulance point. Large bodies of troops were assembled and dispersed here. There was considerable enemy air activity during forenoon, less pronounced during afternoon. Road from IMVROS to escarpment was reported unusable owing to air activity.

p.m.:   LAYFORCE withdrew from IMVROS through ravine and established flank guard at mouth. Ravine, caves and village of COMITIADIS were full of stragglers most of them in a pitiable condition of hunger, exhaustion and disorganisation.

30 May: LAYFORCE remained in defensive positions.

p.m.:   Col. LAYCOCK visited CREFORCE, now established in cave at foot of SPHAKION RAVINE. General FREYBERG defined order of evacuation as fighting troops before stragglers. LAYFORCE to leave last of fighting troops.

31 May
1400:   LAYFORCE relieved on flank by MAORIS and ordered to take up new positions covering town and beach of SPHAKION at mouth of SPHAKION RAVINE.

Final orders from CREFORCE for evacuation (a) LAYFORCE positions not to be held to last man and round but only as long as was necessary to cover withdrawal of other fighting forces. (b) No withdrawal before order from HQ. (c) LAYFORCE to embark after other fighting forces but before stragglers.

2100:   Maj Gen WESTON dictated to BM LAYFORCE orders for capitulation to take effect dawn 1 June. Lt Col COLVIN detailed to present capitulation to enemy.

2200:   On finding that entire staff of CREFORCE had withdrawn, Col LAYCOCK, accompanied by BM and IO proceeded to SPHAKION to obtain authority for withdrawal.

On finding that entire staff of CREFORCE had embarked, in view of fact that all fighting forces were now in position for embarkation and that there was no enemy contact, Col LAYCOCK on his own authority, issued orders to Lt Col YOUNG to lead troops to SPHAKION by route avoiding the crowded main approach to town and to use his own personality to obtain priority laid down in Div orders.

LAYFORCE reached SPHAKION outskirts in good time for boats but were unable to penetrate rabble; flank dets. were able to reach beach but main body remained ashore. Col LAYCOCK, accompanied by BM and IO embarked HMS KIMBERLEY.

Orders for the Capitulation of Crete as given by Major General E. C. Weston Royal Marines on the Evening of 31 May 1941

Version One – as recalled by Lt-Colonel (then Major and Brigade Major Layforce) F.C.C. Graham Argylls in 1948

To: Lt Col Colvin
In view of the following facts:

1. I am informed that RN can carry out no further evacuation after tonight 31 May.
2. That the W/T to GHQ Cairo has failed.
3. That no air support is available.
4. Ammunition and food stocks are exhausted.

I order you to go forward at first light and capitulate to the enemy.

Version Two – as recorded in HQ Layforce War Diary (PRO WO 218/166)

To: Lt Col Colvin
In view of the following facts:

(a) My orders direct me to give preference to evacuation to fighting troops. This has reduced the active garrison below what is required for resistance.
(b) As no rations are left this Saturday night most of the troops are too weak owing to shortage of food and heavy strain to organise further resistance.
(c) The wireless will give out in a few hours and the risk of waiting for instructions from Mideast cannot be accepted as this will leave the Officer Commanding without guidance as to his course of action.
(d) There is no possibility of further evacuation.

I hereby order you to collect what senior officers are available before tomorrow and communicate the gist of this order to them. I further order you to go forward at first light to-morrow and capitulate to the enemy.

Version Three – as received by Lt Col G.A.D. Young, Commanding D Battalion Layforce, at 0300 hours 1 June 1941

To: Senior officer left on the island
Position must be considered in the light of the following facts:

1. There are no more rations and the men have had no food for three days.
2. The wireless set can only last a few more hours and risk of waiting further orders from HQME cannot be accepted.
3. The decision to give priority to withdrawal to fighting troops has reduced numbers below the minimum necessary for resistance.
4. No further evacuation is possible.

You are to collect as many senior officers as possible and make known to them the contents of this order.
You are ordered to make contact with the enemy and arrange capitulation.

Irregular Warfare
Suggestions for the Organisation and Employment of Commandos

(Paper written by Major J.A.R. Milman in April 1943 as a result of his experiences with the Middle East Commandos and Mission 204)

Introduction

1. Any discussion of the application of irregular warfare must be of a controversial nature. This is so because this aspect of warfare occupies no place and little attention in the peace-time curriculum of our Regular Army. And so, when in war the potential value of such forms of warfare becomes apparent under many and diverse conditions, these methods are subject to hasty improvisation. It is the purpose of this article to show by various examples the results leading from this and to suggest means of benefiting from these experiences. I must, however, emphasize that the substance of this article refers only to events and conditions outside the home theatre and does not concern itself with any situation existing there.

2. Commandos or, to use a more comprehensive and definitive term, special service units have been before the public and military eye for upwards of three years. They have been employed on many and diverse tasks in all theatres of war. Yet, while their exploits appeared glamorous to the public in a dark period of the war, they have remained in obscurity as far as the army is concerned. In military circles little is known of their function, less of their potential uses. In many ways the publicity given them has done more harm than good. In this fourth year of war they are still organised on an improvised basis. Operations which may be classified in the commando category are still being carried out by a variety of unco-ordinated and individual organisations. All this while other and newer corps have appeared and taken their place in the army as such. This article therefore is written to draw attention to certain aspects of the employment of commandos because:-

(a) During a period of over two years in commandos abroad the organisation for this form of warfare overseas was, in my experience, basically unsound.

(b) Of the necessity for general co-ordination and planning on a wide basis in any future application of irregular warfare methods.

(c) Attention should be drawn to certain factors in connection with its application to eastern theatres.

(d) In the past, productive results from the employment of commandos has been prejudiced by misunderstanding as to their proper function.

(e) Such defects in organisation as have handicapped past efforts should be placed on record.

3. The conclusions of this article are based on two years active employment on irregular operations with British troops, in three separate theatres of war. That these operations have previously only achieved limited success is, in my opinion, primarily due to the non-observance of the most elementary principles in the system of command and control, resulting in a defective and ineffective higher control organisation. I am pessimistic that the further application of irregular warfare may continue under many of those handicaps, some of which are illustrated in the attached notes. Given effective co-ordination of effort and control in future, I am convinced that this form of warfare could not only pay a high dividend in operations against the Japanese but would play an effective part in the waging of an offensive campaign.

4. Finally, since few staff or regimental officers have any background of knowledge as to the conduct, capabilities and limitations of irregular warfare as carried out by special service units, I have put forward these conclusions in the hope that they may help in a clearer understanding of the subject.

Security
5. I deal first with the security aspect, because its effect on policy has had an unfortunate and overriding influence in the past. Although publicity, such as was accorded the appearance of commandos, appeals to the public, it is inherent in the service to regard the subject of such publicity with dislike and suspicion. This publicity resulting in an estrangement from the remainder of the

army, did the commandos a dis-service. It placed them on a plane to which they had no pretentions for there is nothing abnormal about commandos except that they represent new methods and changed conditions of war. I shall now endeavour to show how an unintelligent application of security can lead to ignorance, obstruction, lack of confidence and biased antagonism resulting finally in frustrated effort.

6.   Dislike and suspicion was further enhanced by another factor. While the press presented the commandos to the public in glorified terms, their development within the service took place in an atmosphere of secrecy and seclusion. Thus, in the midst of the army grew up an organisation of which little was known of its objects and methods, except that it was given an unwarranted amount of public favour. This divorcement of commandos from military matters in general led to unfortunate results because it meant that commanders and staffs had little or no knowledge as to their scope or proper form of employment. For when later, commandos were placed under the control of lower formations, they were generally employed wrongly as the commander had not the requisite knowledge at his disposal. Consequently, many operations were ineffective in results, mistrust deepened, the value of commandos appeared questionable, while their continued favourable publicity led to further resentment. A particular complaint was that the operations carried out by the commandos could have been equally well undertaken by ordinary units. This will be alluded to again later, but the point to be emphasised here is that the grounds for this complaint would not have existed but for the lack of knowledge of commanders and staffs as to the capabilities and limitations of commandos; for the functions of commandos was not intended to include tasks within the capacity of ordinary units for which they were less suitably organised and equipped.

7.   Secrecy and security with regard to commandos should not be stretched therefore beyond the point where co-operation and good relations with the rest of the service may be prejudiced. If security is limited to operational requirements the value of commandos will be seen in its true perspective; and their operational capabilities and limitations will be understood by all. A higher degree of secrecy can in fact only be justified if it is intended to centralise operational control permanently. If such control is to be decentralised, then it is essential that sufficient information regarding the function of any special service units involved is disseminated to the commanders of

staffs concerned. An example of the result of failure to observe this stipulation can be quoted from the Burma campaign of 1941–42. In the autumn of 1941 an irregular warfare organisation was concentrated at a trg centre in Burma named the Bush Warfare School for purposes of cover. This organisation was intended to operate in China and had in fact, no special qualifications for such warfare as its cover name suggested; control, other than for local administration, was exercised by the War Office direct. When war started Burma army obtained the release of certain components of this organisation for operations under its control in Burma. Those components were in fact only cadres of officers and other ranks each totalling about ten officers and fifty other ranks and organised, equipped, and trained to fill a particular role. Any departure from this special function required fundamental alterations; moreover, once separated from their parent organisation no provision for maintenance or for replacement of wastage was possible. Yet they were required to operate as complete and independent units as they stood. It is difficult to assume otherwise than that demands of security resulted in the Burma military authorities being ignorant of essential details and that a wrong appreciation of the operational capacity of these units was made as a consequence.

Employment of Commandos
8.   The scope of commandos vis-a-vis the ordinary infantry unit has already been commented upon to the effect that they are less capable of carrying out the functions of an ordinary infantry unit than the unit itself, and that their employment on such tasks in the past has been a mistake; a fact due to differences of organisation and equipment which must be accepted. Commandos therefore, should not be employed in such a role unless operational necessity demands, when due allowance must be made, as in any improvised arrangement.

9.   The value of commandos in their own sphere can be most truly appreciated against the background into which they came into existence. From this their natural line of evolution and potential uses can be more readily appreciated. The formation of commandos took place to meet the needs of the moment. Dunkirk had crippled our power for offensive action, while the Army at home was primarily concerned in making good its deficiencies in training and equipment for defence against invasion. It was in these circumstances that a force of volunteers was formed to restore in some small degree, our

capacity to carry war to the enemy. Dictated by geographical necessity, these operations involved the development of a new technique which in turn provided the information necessary to perfect the methods for combined operations on a major scale. Employment of commandos in the conditions peculiar to the home theatre has been progressive and continuous.

10.   Although commandos were originally intended for a particular role in amphibious operations – for which they must always be prepared and trained – the definition that commandos are 'a military force formed explicitly to take advantage of Sea Power' presents however, an inaccurate idea, since it presupposes sea-borne operations only. That the scope of commandos is not restricted within this definition is shown by the fact that simultaneously with their evolution at home, commandos were raised in the Middle East, and as other war fronts have opened, the formation of commandos has continued locally; while in these theatres, operations have been very largely restricted to activities requiring an overland approach.

11.   The creation of commandos in each of the various theatres of war leads to the assumption that scope for this kind of warfare exists on a large scale, is a fact that has won universal acceptance. That the extent of this scope may not have been appreciated fully to date, is due primarily to mistakes in organisation and employment arising from the lack of peace time training in, or thought on the subject. An examination of experience gained can remedy this, while consideration of the object of commandos will provide a basis for this thought. It will at the same time expose an argument which is frequently put forward to the effect that the operations of commandos could be carried out equally well by the ordinary infantry unit. For a commando is a unit specially created to carry out irregular operations which may be defined as operations beyond the scope of the normal tactical organisation. The reasons for using special troops instead of ordinary infantry units may be summarised as follows:

(a)   That each theatre of war provides a varying scope for irregular operations of a specialised nature.
(b)   That it is uneconomical to divert regular units to these tasks because of the modifications necessary in training and organisation, and because they are fundamentally part of higher formations.
(c)   The scope of irregular operations requires an elasticity in

organisation and training which it would be impracticable to
super-impose on an ordinary unit.

The fact is, that the scope for irregular operations in any theatre of
war is so great that the ordinary unit, if employed, would rapidly lose
its identity as such, and would cease to fulfil its normal functions. But
commandos should not be regarded as specialists within a narrow
interpretation of the word. They must be capable of operating under
a great variety of conditions, both by sea and land.

12.   The object of commandos therefore, is to provide means of
carrying out operations which are beyond the capacity of ordinary
units, without drastic alteration in their organisation, while the main
principle to be observed in following this object is, that commandos
should not be required to carry out operations which are within the
capacity of the ordinary unit.

Forms of Irregular Warfare
13.   An elaboration of the term 'irregular operation' appears to be
relevant at this stage. The employment of large forces in battle is
governed by more or less stereotyped forms of manoeuvres and
tactics. Irregular warfare consists of evolving methods by which the
enemy may be surprised and any weakness exploited at a low cost.
These methods are usually far removed from the normal tactical
operation and are not directed against the enemy forward troops.
Such operations fall roughly into the following categories:

(a)   Guerrilla operations of a military nature carried out by the local
       population, e.g. levies.
(b)   Irregular operations carried out by specially trained army
       personnel, i.e. commandos or independent companies.

Sabotage and operations of a non-military nature such as those
carried out by agents, fifth columnists etc., are not included here,
but, and particularly in eastern theatres, commando sub-units
might well be used to bolster up such activities. Other aspects of
these activities will be referred to elsewhere.
     The chief target of both classes is the enemy L of C and rear areas.
Their separate functions might be defined as:-

(a)   The object of guerrilla operations is to harass enemy rear lines of
       communications.

(b) The object of commandos etc., is to harass enemy forward lines of
communications behind the battle area or where it is impossible to
employ guerrillas.

The fighting value of guerrillas will vary according to a number of
local considerations, political and physical, but their value as a
source of information will always be considerable if properly
supervised. The value of commandos in eastern theatres may well be
enhanced in both these spheres because of the difficulty in raising
reliable guerrillas or of employing paratroops in jungle country.

But the true value of irregular warfare is perhaps demonstrated
most forcibly by considering the points of contact of the main forces
on either side in relation to their separate responsibilities for defence
over the whole theatre of war. These points of contact are few and
limited in extent. Beyond these limits lies a wide area for irregular
operations which must prove at least an embarrassment if they do
not in fact compel the enemy to a considerable dispersion of force.

Examples of Misemployment
14. Reference has already been made to the fact that commandos
have no firm constitution, and that they appear to be condemned
permanently to the limitations imposed by improvisation. I propose
to show this reliance on improvisation – reflected in the inadequate
machinery set up for higher control and direction – has also
contributed towards the mis-employment and wastage of commandos, and has resulted on occasions in employment evidencing a lack
of clarity as to the purpose for which they were formed. Examples of
this can be instanced from personal experience in both the Middle
East and Burma theatres.

15. On the Gallabat front in the Sudan, control of a commando
was delegated to the local commander. It was used to occupy a sector
of the line and to carry out normal fighting patrols at the expense of
operations against the Italian L of C to Gondar. Later, commandos
performed a purely infantry function in fighting a rearguard action
from Suda Bay to Sphakia during the evacuation of Crete. Other
aspects of their employment in this theatre are quoted elsewhere in
this article.

16. In Burma a commando was formed, and then disbanded prior
to the start of the war with Japan. As a result on the outbreak of
hostilities, commando troops which had been concentrated in
Burma from other theatres for a particular purpose, were diverted at

the last moment to operate in conditions for which they were not designed or organised; and were committed to operations, the control of which rested with staff officers who did not properly understand their special function or the modifications made necessary on account of local conditions.

17.   It appears therefore, that there has been a tendency to regard commandos as a desirable commodity and to create them without first considering their function in relation to the local conditions. The results of this penchant for forming special service units on an ad-hoc basis will be seen later.

Factors Affecting Employment of Commandos

18.   While the methods of applying irregular warfare may vary according to the conditions prevailing in the separate war theatres, one common factor is the aim to strike the enemy at points beyond the reach of the rest of the army; and thus to assist the main effort, either by containing a relatively greater proportion of enemy troops on protective duties than could be opposed by an equivalent number of troops in the field, or by diversionary attacks at vital points away from the battle area, preferably co-ordinated with a major operation elsewhere. Many opportunities for implementing this form of warfare have already been taken in this war; others have been missed.

19.   In the former category can be placed the raids from England on the occupied countries, and also the operations in Libya, both sea-borne and by the L.R.D.G. Unfortunately the stage of the war during which these operations might have been singularly effective co-incided with shortages in equipment which handicapped operations. Who can say what local success might have resulted had commandos, equipped with small launches struck, during 1940–41 at southern Italy, or the Libyan L of C from Malta, instead of from Alexandria in the large craft provided, which precluded surprise. Or what effect well organized raids on the Italian L of C straggling for ninety miles through barren hostile country from Gondar to Metemma might have had; or in Burma, had we possessed the ability and forces with which to counter-infiltrate against the Japanese, which is mainly what irregular warfare implies. For whether the objective is approached by sea or over land, this form of warfare directed at the enemies' back areas and disconnected as it is in terms of space from the operations of the main forces, is one of infiltration.

20.   In operations of this nature, the question of approach to the selected objective is of first importance and may be the chief factor in conditioning the scope of the operation. For where there is a long land approach through enemy controlled territory, the security of the force, particularly in its withdrawal, will depend on its mobility. This in turn, is dependent on the size and ease of control of the force, so that long range penetration tasks may be limited to the employment of small parties, and the tasks must be selected accordingly; while bigger operations can be planned where the line of withdrawal is shortened and security increased.

21.   It is not possible to lay down the detailed organisation for an operation in a review of this nature, as this will always be dictated by a variety of local considerations, among which the demands of mobility, striking power and maintenance, require careful judgement. In general, however, sea-borne operations involve only a short land approach and are a lesser problem than the approach for an overland operation. Nevertheless, the problem of approach is a deciding factor in considering the scope of any operations.

Employment of Commandos in Eastern Theatres
22.   Various attempts to employ commandos or similar troops, in an eastern theatre have already been made. These attempts may be regarded as experiments which do not appear to have reached a conclusive stage yet, either in the elaboration of technique, or in the sphere of strategical planning. As in any other military subject, neither is subject to dogma; in fact, no branch of military thought allows more scope for ingenuity. Therefore, consideration of the possible scope of irregular operations, and the lines on which they might most readily develop in eastern theatres, requires attention.

23.   The opportunity to subject the large area under Japanese occupation to sea-borne attack by commandos in co-operation with the navy seems self-evident in the geographical aspect, while the execution of such operations does not seem to involve any new or particular problems prior to landing; but the conditions with which I now deal are likely to prevail thereafter. Again one must emphasise the principle that the use of commandos should be restricted to operations to which it is uneconomical to divert, or which are beyond the capacity of ordinary infantry units; and that the length of overland approach must be the determining factor in the size of the force used. Such tasks may well be a preliminary to a landing on a major scale.

24.   The scope for overland operations, however, does present peculiar problems. These problems are inherent in the conditions of jungle warfare, to the application of which we have shown, to date, no special aptitude or liking.

Factors Affecting Operations in Jungle Warfare
25.   The problems which jungle country impose on the tactics and conduct of operations, are chiefly connected with the deployment control and supply of large bodies of troops. The jungle imposes unusual limitations on the handling of large formations, even when their organisation is modified and adapted to these conditions. They are tied, to lesser or greater degree, to a long and vulnerable L of C. They are unwieldy and difficult to control. Their mobility is reduced. For these reasons therefore, it is difficult for them to apply their concentrated strength rapidly, or to protect themselves against a form of attack which may result in disorganisation out of all proportion to its scale. The question of mobility is an outstanding problem in jungle warfare. Many factors affect it, but possibly the most important is size. The very factors which limit the effectiveness of large forces, increase the attainment of surprise; mobility is, perhaps, increased rather than reduced; while interference with the process of control is relatively less.

26.   In general the characteristics of the jungle are more favourable to fighting of an independent nature to an elastic plan, than to operations requiring detailed planning, co-ordination and timing. Here, small forces can outwit, out-manoeuvre and out-fight a larger enemy. Here, too, the gun and the tank are at a discount and the rifle, bayonet, grenade and sub-machine gun – the essence of the individual – come into their own. Large formations which alone can consolidate ground won, are dependent on intricate supply services and focal centres in rear. These are the sources where attack may be most felt, and which are hardest to protect. They are the targets for infiltration, but they are beyond the capacity of the ordinary unit to reach. Are they not worthy of special attention? Could not results be expected, proportionately greater than the inroads on manpower required? Do not such tasks require special training, methods, equipment and planning? These questions may well be considered in relation to Japanese methods, and to the defeats inflicted in the jungle on superior British forces.

27.   The value of irregular operations in jungle warfare may be said to lie, therefore, in the facts that:

(a) Penetration behind the enemy front can be easily effected.
(b) The deployment of large numbers of troops has many limitations.
(c) Communications are canalised, long and vulnerable.
(d) The enemy is not able to exercise effective control over the country flanking the axis of his communications.
(e) The value of superiority in armament is reduced.
(f) Advantages are conferred on the operations of small units, particularly in concealment and mobility.

All these considerations lead to the employment of infiltration tactics – methods at which the Japanese have consistently outwitted us, not by the elaboration of a complicated technique but a correct appreciation of simple tactics.

Factors Affecting Infiltration Tactics
28. Here, it is perhaps as well to differentiate between infiltration and an outflanking movement. Under suitable conditions, it may be possible to move a brigade, perhaps more, on an outflanking movement of limited scope, but by infiltration is meant penetration to great depths and for long duration. The application of infiltration tactics by ordinary formations is not practicable for the following reasons:-

Firstly, it requires drastic modification in equipment and unit organisation. Secondly, the conditions of jungle warfare, impose limitations on the size of force which can be readily employed on infiltration tasks. Thirdly, it results in a breaking down of the system of command and control, because even assuming the employment of as large a force as one Bn., the system of brigade control in the normal sense, collapses. Fourthly, provision of aircraft is a special effort which cannot be invariably applied, nor can it solve the problem of maintenance under all conditions.

The nature of these operations pre-supposes also, elasticity in planning far exceeding that permissible in a normal operation. The exact form of the operation may only clarify after leaving the base, and it is necessary that the widest latitude may be permitted the commander in carrying out his instructions. Such freedom of action is hardly practicable in the employment of units in field formations.

29. So far the argument has been directed to showing that the employment of field formations or units however adapted and modified, on infiltration tasks is unsuitable. If this view is accepted, it is still only of negative value. It is therefore necessary to show that

their employment in this form is uneconomical. What is the object of such methods? Briefly, they aim at:-

(a) Drawing enemy forces away from the vital point by containing them on L of C protection or elsewhere.
(b) Dislocating the enemy L of C and rear areas.
(c) Destruction of enemy V.P.s [Vital Points].

Now on all, except very rare occasions, the above tasks can be carried out by much smaller forces than a brigade, and as we have seen, the necessity of using limited force may be determined by the conditions effecting the approach.

Further, to carry out such operations for any length of time, using units of formations is to divert them from their proper tasks of opposing the enemy's main forces. It also imposes the control of such operations on the staff, and where the scope is extensive, this can only be satisfactorily co-ordinated at a high headquarters. The incorporation of commando or guerrilla units in the establishment of a division is not really an adequate solution as the extent of their operational capacity is thereby localised and reduced; while, in fact, the scope for irregular operations ranges far and wide beyond the immediate battle area. It seems therefore that the responsibility of formations for infiltration tasks should be strictly limited, and that behind the line stipulated, responsibility should devolve on a higher headquarters.

Higher Direction of Irregular Warfare and Subversive Operations
31.   If it is accepted that there is scope for such operations, directed at the enemy's communications, and that they require a different technique and planning, which is outside the experience of most commanders and staffs, then control by a special headquarters and staff becomes necessary for productive results. In order to co-ordinate the prosecution of irregular warfare over the whole theatre of war general control should be vested in one authority; this headquarters should occupy status commensurate with this requirement. On the surface, the creation of a special headquarters and staff may seem unnecessary and impracticable, but when one considers that these operations are not necessarily concerned with the situation in the battle area, whether this be offensive, defensive, static or mobile, but can be carried on independently of, or in co-ordination with the situation there as conditions may demand, then the value of this arrangement is more evident.

The argument is further strengthened when it is considered that the control and direction of commandos has normally been superimposed on some department of the staff as additional to their normal responsibilities. Owing to the extent of the scope of irregular operations this arrangement is quite inadequate and this factor alone has contributed largely to past mismanagement.

31.   It is now necessary to define the function of this headquarters more clearly. Since it can be seldom, if ever feasible, or necessary to employ commandos concentrated on a formation basis the function of this headquarters is not one of direct control over individual operations but is limited to strategic planning and to the selection of objectives; and to the detailing of the force for a particular operation. The responsibility for detailed operational planning must be left to the commando unit selected to carry out the operation. Each commando unit must therefore be regarded as a separate entity rather than as part of a higher formation; and similarly sub-units within units. An analogy can perhaps be made with bomber operations in which a bomber mission represents a commando operation, control and direction being exercised by Bomber Command and Commando HQ respectively. This HQ can be, therefore, a semi-static organisation, exercising, within the limits prescribed by higher policy, an independent control relative to the 'G' staff.

33.   Attention has already been drawn to the fact that irregular operations are being carried out all the time by a variety of independent organisations. Many of them, guerrillas, levies etc., are not commandos in the sense of those commandos which are composed of military personnel; but they are off-shoots of the same tree. But the system whereby the control of these organisations has been decentralised variously under separate branches of the staff or even under various government departments can, viewed as a whole, scarcely be said to have produced results which accorded with the expenditure in money, time and effort, whatever its other commendations. It must and in fact has lead to overlapping and duplication of effort between the various departments concerned and their separate organisations. Economy of effort and proper co-ordination can be achieved only if control of these separate organisations is subject to centralised direction.

34.   Such organisations, therefore, together with 'fifth column' and similar organisations should be included within the sphere of this

special headquarters and staff. Thus if this was set up in India as a Directorate of Irregular Warfare and Subversive Operations, organised on a basis of geographical areas similar to the War Office intelligence system, direct control could be exercised over all irregular operations, and plans could be adjusted to normal military requirements when close co-operation may be desired. In this circumstance a representative of the Directorate should be attached to the HQ of the formation concerned in an advisory capacity to ensure proper application of the commando effort. In this way all irregular forms of warfare could be co-ordinated over the whole theatre of operations within an objective plan.

35.   It seems relevant at this point to draw attention to a misconception which appears to me to be responsible for much of the confusion that has existed heretofore. The tendency to regard irregular warfare as beyond the scope of the professional soldier and as the special province of civilians is to be deprecated. For whatever their form, irregular operations are operations of war and as such require a sound military judgement in organisation and planning to which all other aspects, however important, should be subordinated; only when the specialised local knowledge of civilians is allied to military technique can maximum effectiveness be achieved. Whilst the inclusion of civilians in an advisory capacity is obviously necessary, if control and direction of irregular warfare were to be placed in the hands of experienced military personnel, this would lead to a greater efficiency in the spheres of organisation, administration and planning, which would be reflected in the conduct and results of operations.

Example of a Commando Role
36.   An example of the practical application of a commando under jungle conditions might be as follows:-

It has already been stated in jungle warfare, that communications with local fronts are generally long and vulnerable. Long stretches of indefensible road, flanked by jungle are interspersed with the usual L of C installations. The detailed location and state of this L of C may not be ascertainable by air recce. Such information can be easily obtained by ground recce on account of the concealment afforded by the jungle. Long range ground recce is itself of great value, but is it not also within our power to make the maintenance of this L of C difficult and costly to the enemy. To effect this consistent pressure is necessary. This can be maintained economically only if we base our operations in enemy country, and co-ordinate pressure on his L of C sector by sector. The practicability of such methods depends on:-

(a) The lack of control exercised by the enemy over the country as a whole.
(b) The hostility of the local population to the enemy, or the depopulated nature of the countryside.

Such conditions exist in eastern theatres today. The application of these methods requires therefore:-

(a) The establishment of small mobile operational bases on a line parallel to the enemy L of C but beyond reasonable striking distance of his protective detachments.
(b) The allotment to the bases of operational zones; sufficiently large to ensure that small mobile parties can avoid being pinned down.

The phasing of such an operation might be:-

(a) Allotment of operation area and general objective.
(b) Operation area prepared for occupation by reconnaissance and possibly propaganda.
(c) Detachment occupies area.

This is only one example of the possible employment of commando troops on infiltration tasks, which is quoted because its effect on the operations of the main forces is most obvious. Whether such tasks are land-based or sea-borne is immaterial for the essential factors in the eastern theatre remain the same and the scope may well be restricted only by the limitation in vision of the commander and staff, or the resources available. The ability of commandos to carry out special tasks in jungle warfare derives from their mobility and elasticity in organisation. This allows them to be used as a screen ahead of the more unwieldly formations with the object of securing local domination of the jungle.

Organisation of Commandos
37.   In considering the most suitable organisation for commandos a review of the past shows various defects. The argument for vesting control of operations in a special headquarters has already been put forward on the grounds that the diversion of commandos from their proper role in the past, has been due primarily to this mission; and to

the consequent delegation of responsibility for their employment to local formation commanders.

38.   The tactical organisation of commando units must be designed to achieve a flexibility capable of adaption to the variety of operations which come within their scope – that is, to any operation by sea or land which is beyond the normal capacity of the ordinary infantry unit. For example an objective such as Bomba, an Italian sea-plane base on the coast of Cyrenaica, necessitated detailed planning and an attack in force by a complete commando; whereas in the Sudan long distance harassing operations directed through thick bush country against the Italian road, L of C required the employment of small commando sub-units operating independently.

Deficiencies in armament and supporting fire have to be counter-balanced by individualism and by surprise, mobility and the use of short range assault weapons. Each sub-unit down to the smallest division must be self contained and capable of operating alone. But in all spheres, economy must be a key note to organisation. No remarks on the tactical organisation of commandos can be concluded without a reference to the necessity for special local knowledge for these operations. Where, therefore, commandos are introduced into new and unfamiliar conditions, provision of that local knowledge by the attachment of qualified officers and civilians and probably local inhabitants as well, as guides and interpreters.

39.   An inherent weakness in organisation has been the problem of maintaining units and replacing wastages. The system whereby personnel are obtained from ordinary units is not satisfactory for many and obvious reasons. It should suffice to say by way of illustration that the disbandment of SS units has sometimes been due to the lack of normal means of replacing wastage. The most satisfactory answer to this would be a direct intake of recruits at home, and the holding of reinforcements at depots abroad. In other words, the establishment of commandos on a corps basis.

This would also eliminate all the internal administrative difficulties which have been symptomatic of the improvised organisation of commandos to date; of which an example in point is the unsatisfactory system whereby pay accounts of men transferred to commandos remain with their respective regimental paymasters. Besides throwing a terrific and unnecessary strain on the reduced administrative resources provided in an SS unit it has invariably resulted in loss of touch with the majority of these pay offices, so that no information has been available on accounts for the correctness of which the unit commander is responsible; whilst also imposing a degree of hardship on the troops. The placing of commandos on a regularised footing would eliminate such problems. It would also obviate such a situation as occurred when volunteers to proceed to Burma were called for in the Middle East. As an inducement GHQ ME officially announced special rates of pay for this party. But on arrival in Burma these terms were repudiated. Although they would not have affected the issue of volunteering with the troops in question the point of this case should be considered relative to my previous remarks on organisation in general.

It would allow too for a common doctrine and basis of training and for co-ordination between the various theatres of war; and it would enable commandos to function on an army or empire wide basis as the scope for their employment seems to demand. In view of the complexity of equipment and organisation of modern infantry, it might even result in their expansion into a new and complementary form of light infantry, achieving that general elasticity in organisation and methods so essential to warfare in the eastern theatre, and of supplying that assistance to the field formations for which they are looking.

But unless some such system is introduced a situation prevails as in India today where numerous commando officers and men have arrived, as stragglers from operational areas overseas, to find no organisation exists into which they could be absorbed. Unwanted, they have been allowed to drift and valuable experience and training is going to waste. That this state of affairs can exist reflects on the system which lacking a consistent policy and observing no semblance of continuity permits special service units to be created and broken up in accordance with the fluctuating demands of rapidly changing situations.

It is impossible to pass over the matter of recruiting without touching on a very vexed question – the question of the standard below which a man is not fit for this kind of service. At a time when all arms are pressing their claims on account of the increasing introduction of technical equipment difficulty in according rights of priority in this respect is obvious. Nevertheless if it is decided to conduct such operations, then their nature requires a high degree of intelligent initiative on the part of the individual as well as a sense of personal responsibility beyond the limits of normal discipline.

Conclusion

40.   In conclusion the various points connected with the organisation and employment of commandos may be summarised as follows:-

(a)   The object of commandos is the prosecution of operations beyond the capacity of ordinary field units, and for which they should be reserved.

(b)   These operations have a potential value in the eastern theatre of war, their object being to contain enemy forces with a minimum expenditure of troops.

(c)   The value of commandos can only be fully realised if they are employed on operations for which they are specifically created.

(d)   The strategical application of irregular operations can be co-ordinated most effectively if controlled by a special staff.

(e)   The tactical organisation of commandos requires flexibility, and unit commanders' maximum freedom in the execution of orders.

(f)   Operations should aim at penetrating enemy territory to as great a depth as possible, remembering that the conditions governing the approach decide the size of the force for any operation.

(g)   The efficient control of commandos requires their organisation on a corps basis.

(h)   Clarity as to the purpose for which commandos are to be used is essential to planning and to the execution of plans.

(i)   Co-operation and mutual regard between commandos and the remainder of the army is facilitated if security and secrecy conform with operational necessity only.

41.   Finally, such operations as this article envisages may not be of decisive value in each instance; but if the eastern theatre of war is examined objectively in relation to the opportunity for exploiting the many and various forms of irregular warfare, against targets both within and without the immediate battle area, then the cumulative effect of the employment of commandos, independent companies, or other irregular warfare organisations, in a well-conceived strategic plan, may well be a decisive factor in warfare against the Japanese.

I realise that to apply the suggestions I have put forward in their entirety may well be an impracticable proposition at this stage; but if the substance of my arguments is accepted then much can be done to improve the situation in a modified way. If this article succeeds in placing before commanders and staffs a new view of some of the factors connected with the application of irregular warfare it will have achieved its purpose; and obstructive barriers which have existed, and to a great extent impaired the commando effort in the past, so far as my experience is concerned, will have been removed.

April 43   (sgd)   Major
Quetta   (J.A.R. MILMAN)

Members and Former Members of the Middle East Commando Historical Research Group

Len Addicott (No. 50)
Wiggy Andrews (Nos. 50, 50/52)
Harry Beedell (Nos. 50, 50/52)
The Late Colonel Michael Borwick DL (Nos. 50, 50/52)
Leighton Bowen (Nos. 50, 50/52)
Captain Archie Cochrane CBE (No. 50/52)
H.L. Collins (No. 51)
Tim Darby (Nos. 50, 50/52)
E. Darling (No. 52)
Jacob Domb (No. 51)
Juan Garcia (Nos. 50, 50/52)
Colonel Philip Keymer MC (No. 51)
Major Bob McGibbon (Nos. 50, 50/52)
Lt-Colonel John Milman OBE (Nos. 52, 50/52)
The Late Brigadier Jack Monteith CBE MC (No. 50)
The Late Arthur Noble (Nos. 50, 50/52)
Lt-Colonel Stephen Rose OBE (Nos. 50, 50/52)
Harry Scholfield (Nos. 52, 50/52)
Major William Seymour (Nos. 52, 50/52)
Aryeh Shay (No. 51)
Dick Sheehy (No. 50)
Colonel David Smiley MVO OBE MC (No. 52)
Zvi Svet (No. 51)
Captain Arthur Swinburn DCM (Nos. 50, 50/52)
George Williams (Nos. 50, 50/52)
Colonel George Young DSO (Nos. 50, 52, 50/52)

Honorary Members
John Cator (son of Lt-Colonel Henry Cator MC of No. 51)
Nancy Furlong (sister of Captain Henry Frost of No. 51)
Lt-Colonel Charles Messenger
Martin Miller (son of Lt-Colonel C.D.O. Miller of No. 51)
David Pendlebury (son of Captain John Pendlebury)

Source Notes

Chapter One
1. Fox-Davies to Wavell 1 October 1935 from Fergusson, Bernard *Wavell, Portrait of a Soldier* (Collins, 1962).
2. Cator Diary entry 2 February 1940.
3. *Ibid.* 16/17 June 1940.
4. Personal message dated 14 September 1940. Copy in Cator Diary.
5. Cunningham *A Sailor's Odyssey* p. 289.

Chapter Two
1. Smith to OC No. 51 ME Cdo G(R)/M/ VI/13 dated 23 January 1941. Original in Cator Diary.
2. Gilbert Martin, *Finest Hour* pp. 1914–5 (Heinemann, 1983).
3. Nicolson, Harold, *Diaries and Letters Vol 2 1939–1945* p. 148 (Collins, 1983).
4. 9 March 1941. PRO PREM 3/124/1.
5. Letter Brig M.J. D'A Blackman OBE MC to Lt-Colonel S.M. Rose OBE dated 24 January 1983. MECHRG Papers.
6. The report is to be found under PRO ADM 1/11056.
7. PRO WO 169/923.
8. Letter dated 19 March 1941. PRO WO 193/405.

Chapter Three
1. Diary entry 8 March 1941.
2. Letter Directorate Public Relations, War Office to Mrs J. Meadows Frost dated 14 February 1942. Original in MECHRG Papers.
3. Diary entry 15 March 1941.
4. *Ibid.* 17 March 1941.
5. Glover, Michael, *An Improvised War: The Abyssinian Campaign of 1940-1941* pp. 109 ff (Leo Cooper, 1987).
6. Letter dated 25 May 1941, Cator Diary.
7. HQ Troops in the Sudan and Eritrea Operation Instruction No 1 dated 24 June 1941. PRO WO 169/2585.
8. *Ibid.* Operational Instruction No 2.
9. Letter dated 4 July 1941, Cator Diary.

Chapter Four
1. PRO WO 218/172.
2. PRO WO 218/166.
3. PRO WO 218/172.
4. PRO DEFE 2/699.
5. *Ibid.*
6. *Ibid.*
7. PRO WO 218/166

Chapter Five
1. Clarke to Daniell PRO WO 193/405.
2. Churchill, Winston, *The Second World War Vol 3* p. 720.
3. PRO PREM 3/330/9.
4. PRO DEFE 2/699.
5. Colville, John, *The Fringes of Power: Downing Street Diaries 1939–1945* p. 416 (Hodder & Stoughton, 1985).
6. 16 August 1941. Churchill *op. cit.* p. 725.
7. PRO CAB 44/152.
8. *Ibid.*
9. Airey to DDO 1 April 1942. PRO WO 201/732.
10. Minute dated 21 April 1942. *Ibid.*
11. Letter dated 8 August 1942. *Ibid.*
12. Dated September 1942. *Ibid.*

Chapter Six
1. The information for this chapter is drawn from PRO WO 193/602 and WO 209/ 304A, a written account by Lt-Colonel John Milman and comment from William Seymour.

Chapter Seven
1. MOD letter D/PS(A)90/1 PS12 (Army) dated 31 July 1986.

Select Bibliography

Barker, A.J., *Eritrea 1941* (Faber 1966)

Buckley, Christopher, *Greece and Crete 1941* (HMSO 1952)

Churchill, W.S., *The Second World War Vols 2 and 3* (Cassell 1950)

Connell, John, *Wavell, Scholar and Soldier* (Collins 1964)

Cunningham, Admiral of the Fleet The Viscount, *A Sailor's Odyssey* (Hutchinson 1951)

Messenger, Charles, *The Commandos 1940–1946* (Kimber 1985)

Ministry of Information, *The Abyssinian Campaign* (HMSO 1942)

Pitt, Barrie, *The Crucible of War: The Western Desert 1941* (Cape 1980)

Playfair, Major General I.S.O., *A History of the Second World War: The Mediterranean and Middle East* (HMSO 1954)

Rose, Lt-Colonel S.M., Castelorizzo 24–28 February 1941 *(Army Quarterly & Defence Journal* July 1984)

Roskill, Capt Stephen, *Churchill and the Admirals* (Collins 1971)

Seymour, William, *British Special Forces* (Sidgwick & Jackson 1985)

Simpson, Tony, *Operation Mercury* (Hodder & Stoughton 1981)

Stewart, I. McD. G., *The Struggle for Crete, 20 May–1 June 1941* (OUP 1966)

Index

Ranks given are those finally achieved, where known.